The Mystery
of the Ordinary

1817

Harper & Row, Publishers, San Francisco

Cambridge, Hagerstown, New York, Philadelphia

London, Mexico City, São Paulo, Sydney

The Mystery
of the Ordinary

CHARLES CUMMINGS

Grateful acknowledgment is made to the following publishers: Simon & Schuster for excerpts from Aaron Sussman and Ruth Goode, *The Magic of Walking* (1967); New Directions for excerpts from Thomas Merton, trans., *The Way of Chuang-Tzu* (© 1965 by The Abbey of Gethsemani); Cistercian Publications for excerpts from Bernard of Clairvaux, *On the Song of Songs,* translated by Kilian Walsh (1976); Viking Penguin Inc. for excerpts from Peter Matthiessen, *The Snow Leopard* (copyright © 1978 by Peter Matthiessen); Macmillan Publishing Co., Inc., and A. R. Mowbray for excerpts from *The Desert Christian: The Sayings of the Desert Fathers,* translated and with a foreword by Benedicta Ward, S.L.G. (copyright © 1975 by Sister Benedicta); St. Anthony Messenger Press for excerpts from Murray Bodo, O.F.M., *Walk in Beauty* (copyright © 1974 by St. Anthony Messenger Press, 1615 Republic Street, Cincinnati, Ohio 45210. All rights reserved).

Scripture texts used in this work are taken from the *New American Bible,* copyright © 1970 by the Confraternity of Christian Doctrine, Washington, D.C., used by permission of copyright owner. All rights reserved.

FIRST EDITION

Designer: Jim Mennick

Library of Congress Cataloging in Publication Data

Cummings, Charles, 1940-
THE MYSTERY OF THE ORDINARY.

Includes bibliographies.
1. Spiritual life—Catholic authors.   I. Title.

| BX2350.2.C835 | 248.4'82 | 81-47846 |
| ISBN 0-06-061652-0 | | AACR2 |

---

82 83 84 85 86 10 9 8 7 6 5 4 3 2 1

To all who prefer the extraordinary

Contents

. . . .

Preface

. . . .

We may live in extraordinary times, but most of us spend the greater part of our existence doing quite ordinary things. Our simple, everyday experiences can, however, put us in touch with the deepest mystery of life. "Whatever you do," wrote Thomas Merton in an essay called "Learning to Live," "every act, however·small, can teach you everything—provided you see who it is that is acting."* The one who is acting in all our acts is not only the created agent who performs them, but also an uncreated, divine Agent who informs them with his presence and his loving plan for us. Ordinary things have a great power to reveal the mysterious nearness of a caring, liberating God.

Unfortunately, the sameness and repetition of everyday activities can numb our awareness to the point that these ordinary realities no longer speak to us with power. We get nothing out of the ordinary, and so conclude that nothing of value is there. Instead we seek extraordinary experiences and the special techniques that might induce such states. We put religious experience too easily into the category of the unusual, and never expect to find God in the flow of the usual things we do. The rich, spiritual dimension of our ordinary activities is thus lost to us.

To discover the mystery of the ordinary, it is not enough merely to go through the motions of rising, walking, eating, resting, as we have done every day of our life. Going through the motions mechanically and mindlessly is counterproductive. What is helpful is to be gently, attentively present to the full reality of our human experience here and now. Then these ordi-

---

* Thomas Merton, *Love and Living* (New York: Farrar, Straus, Giroux, 1979), p. 14.

nary happenings can become vehicles that carry us towards the mystery of God.

The following chapters examine several ordinary experiences with a sharpened sensitivity. Like Nathanael in the gospel, who at first doubted that anything worthwhile could come from a commonplace village like Nazareth, we "come and see," with simplicity and openness, and then discover "much greater things" in our common daily life than we ever expected to encounter [see John 1:45–51]. The biblical writings of the Judaeo-Christian tradition will light up for us the ultimate possibilities of these ordinary events against the background of the sacred. Once the ordinary has revealed its mystery, the skies may open for us as they did for Nathanael, and we "shall see the angels of God ascending and descending on the Son of Man" [John 1:51].

1 Hearing

. . . .

For most of us the ability to hear, as well as the ability to see, touch, smell, and taste, comes as standard equipment at birth. What is acquired so easily is not always valued highly. When we happen to lose one of our senses through disease, accident, or old age, then we appreciate what used to be there. Recognizing the mystery of the ordinary is partly a matter of attunement to the reality of our human experience while we are still able to appreciate it. The first two chapters will dwell reflectively and appreciatively on hearing and seeing, the most highly developed of our five principal sensing capacities.

Human persons, by their nonmaterial or spirit-level powers of thinking, loving, and choosing in freedom, are beings who transcend the purely material level of reality. Since we are embodied human spirits with bodily senses, we can be in touch with our own totality and with one another and with the world around us through our eyes, ears, nose, taste buds, and skin. As sensate beings, we depend on stimuli from our human and non-human environment in order to function properly at all levels of the self, including the spirit level. We do not manufacture what we know, but know reality as it is, faithfully reflected to us through our senses.

In this view of the human person, the senses and their activity are not demeaned but esteemed. The five primary senses are five doorways through which the world enters the person and the person interacts with the real world. And through the doorways of the senses, as we will discover, it is possible for human persons to approach a relationship with God their creator, a relationship that may eventually go far beyond the sensate without ever losing its rootedness in the realities that we can hear, see, touch, smell, and taste.

The World of Sound

My ears are the doorway to the world of sound. If I disregard for a moment all my other sense impressions and focus my attention on the sounds that surround me, I find myself in a world far more fascinating than I would have guessed. I am intrigued and try to listen more intently so as to distinguish every echo from this world that I usually take for granted and do not really hear.

I am sitting alone in a small room on a warm summer afternoon at the monastery where I live. I suppose the sounds most frequently associated with monasteries might be the tolling of bells and the chanting of psalms. At the moment, all three bells in our tower are silent and there are no church services in progress; but I can hear other sounds coming from outside through the open window, and I can identify familiar sounds from inside the building coming through the door. From outside I hear several different birdsongs and the buzzing wings of a mud dauber wasp, the fountain splashing in the goldfish pond, the squeak of irrigation pipes being twisted apart, the slapping pulsations of the water sprinklers on the lawn and the fields, gasoline or diesel engines in the distance on trucks, tractors, and lawnmower, and overhead a jet aircraft fading rapidly away. The sounds from inside the building seem more pronounced because there is no background music from radio or television to mute them. I hear typewriters and adding machines from the nearby offices, occasional hammering and sawing from the remodeling project on the floor above, doors closing or being pulled open, the muffled murmur of conversation and occasional laughter from the adjacent room, an intercom phone ringing in the abbot's office, monks walking by on the tiled floor with their own distinctive gaits or squeaky shoes, and from the kitchen on the floor below the hiss of steam being released from a cooker and the clatter of pots and pans. My world of sound is a blend of natural and manmade noises. Throughout the day and the night this blend will alter in composition, intensity, and proportion, but there will always be an ambience of sound whenever I wish to listen intently to it.

Filling in the Picture

In my description of the sounds I could hear from my typing room, I supplied both the dynamic element—the sound itself—and the causal element—the sound's source. I recognized "the hiss of steam being released from a cooker, and the clatter of pots and pans" in the kitchen. To know the sound alone—the hiss and clatter—without knowing its source, could be unsettling and intolerable. Sounds such as hisses and clatters demand to be identified before I can be at peace. Unidentified noise can rouse anxiety and sometimes panic; if I hear a sound outside my bedroom window in the middle of the night, I try to identify it. Was it a stray dog or cat, or was it a prowler trying to enter my house? Noise in itself is often ambiguous.

Many sounds that reach the human ear are low in informational content, and their ambiguity must be filled in by the listener to present a more complete and satisfying image. Even human speech can be ambiguous. In a face-to-face conversation, meanings are communicated not simply by sound but in many nonverbal ways, such as facial expression, proximity, gestures, and attitudes. A telephone conversation demands even greater involvement by the listener to fill in a complete picture of the unseen speaker at the other end of the line. Sounds in general, and human speech in particular, trigger a picture-completion process in the listener that brings imagination, memory, emotion, thought, and willing into play.

Hearing is not an activity belonging to the ears alone. I hear not merely with my ears but with my whole self. The sound perceived, especially the word addressed directly to me, integrates various powers and levels of the self in the effort of interpreting and acknowledging the message. If a word of command is addressed to me, I am expected to obey. If the word is an invitation or a call for help, I am expected to respond. If the word is a question, I am expected to answer. Even a casual word calls for a reply in kind. In every case, it is not enough simply to hear the sound; I am expected to do something about it.

Hearing, in the fullest sense, engages the listener's participation. The message received through the ear involves the whole person potentially. Music, for example, can be a totally absorbing experience that resonates far beyond the audio pickup of the ears. A Sousa march can fill the heart from a spirit of pride and patriotism, and set feet tapping and hands clapping in excitement. The music has involved head, heart, hands, and feet, not simply the ears. The advertising industry is aware of the various effects of music on the emotions, and tries to motivate behavior and promote purchasing through appropriate background music. In doctors' and dentists' offices, background music can soothe anxiety and distract from pain. These effects of music are an application of the principle that hearing is an integrating, filling-in activity, not a merely passive, absorbent experience.

How Do We Hear?

The sound that originates in a jet plane thirty thousand feet above me is heard in my brain. The path of the sound waves from the jet to my ears and finally to my brain is an amazing journey. Sound is a vibration of air molecules in a wave pattern of compression followed by rarefaction. What registers in my brain as "roar of a jet engine" is an electrochemical impulse transmitted by the auditory nerve containing data about the pitch, loudness, and timbre of the sound. The function of my ear is to receive, convert, and faithfully transmit the sound of the jet.

The ears of whales, birds, and bats may outperform human ears in their specialized functions, but the human ear is a superbly designed instrument within the ample limits of its range of frequency. Incoming sound waves are channeled by the outer ear into the middle ear, where they activate three small bones that vibrate against the eardrum of the fluid-filled cochlea, or inner ear. Vibrations in the air are converted to vibrations in fluid with minimum loss of intensity. The spiral-shaped inner ear, where the auditory nerve fibers meet the delicate hairlike elements in the cochlear fluid, is protected by a portion of the temporal bone of the skull that is the hardest bony area in the body. The mechanical energy of the sound waves is received by thousands of hair cells that cause electrochemical reactions in the auditory nerve endings, according to the frequency, intensity, and complexity of the sound. Information transmitted to the brain is compared, synthesized, and ultimately "heard."

The human ear is attuned to tiny variations of pitch and intensity. With practice, many people can distinguish a quarter tone on the musical scale, and can perceive the harmonic overtones that separate consonance from dissonance. We can tell whether a sound originates left or right of us because it reaches one ear a few microseconds sooner than the other ear or is a few decibels louder in one ear. By selective attention, the ears can tune in to one or two significant sounds and tune out or tune down all other sounds in the background. For example, we can follow a particular theme as it is played by different sections of the orchestra, or follow a particular instrument while the other instruments and melodies recede into the background. Or we can concentrate on a single speaker or a single conversation in a room filled with the babble of voices.

I have been describing how the ear functions, but have not yet answered the question, "How do we hear?" The preceding section indicated that hearing is an integrating, holistic function that goes beyond the mere reception of sound by the ears. How is it, then, that we are able to hear in the full, and fully involving, sense of the word? Our ability to hear can be understood as the consequence of a basic openness that we enjoy as human beings whether we know it or not. A basic component of our humanity is an openness to the whole of reality, even to its furthest horizon. We exist as human persons ready to take in, to know, to relate to everything that is. Data does not simply bounce off when it reaches us, but is welcomed, taken in, and given a place inside us because our human openness is unlimited, at least in principle. When another person addresses us, his or her word can touch our heart and call forth a response from what is deepest within us; we are able to hear the person's word in this way because of our fundamental human openness.

The fact that we cannot close our ears as we close our eyes by blinking the eyelids may be taken as a sign of our radical openness to the world. If there are sound waves within our range of hearing, we must hear them. Even during sleep, if a jet plane flies over, the sound waves will vibrate our ear drums and stimulate the nerve endings in the labyrinth of the inner ear. However, the sleeping brain usually remains selectively inattentive to all but the most important sounds, such as the alarm clock that we have set or the cries of an infant that awaken its parents. Considering only the ears, their natural mode is always openness and readiness to function. Even before birth the ears are fully formed. The intricate inner ear develops first and is of adult size by the fifth month; the middle and outer ear are operable by the seventh month. In the Islamic Sufi culture, a sheik blows into the ears of a newborn infant to awaken the consciousness within; but the baby is pre-endowed with a relation-seeking, receptive openness to the world.

Being Deaf, By Choice or Otherwise

The openness of the human person to the world is manifested in other sensate and rational functions besides hearing, so that physical deafness does not destroy a basic component of humanness. Nevertheless, deafness is a handicap that has been called by Helen Keller "a much worse misfortune" than blindness. To appreciate the gift of normal hearing it is enough to reflect on the lives of one or two people who experienced total deafness.

Helen Keller, who died in 1968 at the age of eighty-eight, was totally deaf and blind from the age of nineteen months as a result of illness. She considered the problems of deafness to be deeper than those of blindness, because loss of the sound of the human voice means loss of the stimulus that stirs thought and permits the most fulfilling human companionship. Helen Keller managed to break free of her silent, dark, closed world, and to eventually graduate *cum laude* from Radcliffe, thanks to the innate energy of her human spirit and the devoted services of her teacher, Anne Sullivan. The initial breakthrough into systematic forms of communication occurred at age seven, when Helen learned that things have names which can be spelled with the manual alphabet. This dramatic moment of opening and awakening took place with a discovery of the word for water as

Helen experienced the sensation of holding her hand under the gushing pump while her teacher spelled the letters into her other hand. In an instant of intuition, Helen Keller acquired the key to all language. "That living word," she wrote, "awakened my soul, gave it light, hope, joy, set it free!" From that moment she began to act as a free and autonomous self, determined to have her rightful place in the world of those who can hear and see. She learned even how to love music through a tactile sensitivity to the rhythmic beat. On one occasion she began to move in response to the pulsations from the pipe organ in St. Bartholomew's Church. Later she wrote of that experience in her autobiography: "I felt the mighty waves of sound beat against me, as the great billows beat against a little ship at sea."

One of the world's greatest musicians, Beethoven, composed and directed major works for a decade while completely deaf. Beethoven was thirty and had not yet expressed his full musical originality when he began to lose his hearing through the hardening of a bone, a condition that could be arrested or repaired today but could not at the beginning of the nineteenth century. Before he was fifty Beethoven was nearly stone deaf, but his resolute and determined willpower motivated him to continue composing works that were not numerous but were rich and dense in musical thought. His ninth and final symphony accomplished a bold innovation by introducing a choir in the finale to sing Schiller's "Ode to Joy." Beethoven himself, deaf though he was, conducted the opening performance in 1824. He did not know that the audience was applauding until one of the soloists made him turn around to see the appreciation that he could not hear. Three years later Beethoven died, in almost total seclusion.

Withdrawal into oneself often accompanies deafness. Beethoven preferred to avoid the society he could no longer share fully. He was restrained from suicide by the music he felt called upon to produce. Helen Keller sometimes felt left out, and if no one in a group made signs to her for a long period, she would interrupt them to inquire what was being discussed. The deaf may suppose that others are talking about them and become embarrassed. In old age, partial if not total deafness is often the result of nerve deterioration. Low tones are the first to disap-

pear. Voices seem to come from further away. As hearing
grows poorer, the person feels left alone, more and more out of
touch with the world, less able to make the great effort to cross
that gap of soundlessness, yielding eventually to an overbearing
silence. Where there was openness there will be closure and
deafness, unless the process is somehow resisted and reversed.

We have been considering the deafness that comes unbid-
den, as a result of sickness, accident, or old age. The phrase
"turning a deaf ear" reminds us that there is also a deafness that
is freely chosen, or at least apparently so. This kind of deafness
is all the harder to penetrate because it is not always recognized
by those who seem afflicted by it. Who admits his or her deafness, prejudice, closed mindedness? When it seems to others
that we are turning a deaf ear, it seems to us to be superior
wisdom or high principle or admirable firmness. In fact, however, human hearing can be a highly selective, subjective process. We tend to hear what we want to hear, picking out only
the appealing overtones, or creatively supplying them. If we
think highly of a person, we hear good news whenever that
person speaks. Conversely, we tend to be deaf to what we do
not want to hear. The deafness may not be due to ill will, but
the result of selective inattention to data that we cannot incor-
porate into an existing set of values and priorities. For example,
we may turn a deaf ear to signals coming from another generation or expressed in another style of language. Closure is a pro-
tective reaction against a message that is too threatening or
demanding, too disturbing to our lifestyle. If our way of living
is one that deserves to be disturbed and rearranged, then deafness will seal us in a deadly, pointless existence. Instead of a
free, enlivening openness to the whole of reality, there will be a
self-chosen enclosure in loveless meaninglessness. To turn a
deaf ear is ultimately to choose the absurd.

Hearing the Song of Life

Those who choose to turn an open ear to the world should
be able to hear more than mere noise, more than mere sound.
They should be able to hear the song of life that resonates

throughout the created universe and even in their own personal existence. The song of life, and related metaphors, are ways of pointing to the underlying harmony that blends together all persons, events, and objects found in a world that is governed by a caring and provident creator. The open ear is an openness to these mysterious harmonies.

The song of life has analogies with ordinary song or instrumental music, but it has to do with more than audible sounds. A song written by John Denver in 1980, entitled "Song for the Life," tells of listening "for a sound like the sun goin' down." Since the sun goes down inaudibly, the songwriter has chosen an unexpected metaphor that draws our attention to the human capacity to listen very intently and to hear the unexpected. Familiarity with audible musical sound has led the singer to be open to the larger, more lasting rhythms and harmonies of life itself. All creation sings the song of life.

Both in the culture of the East and the culture of the West we find, from the beginning, a sensitivity to cosmic harmony. In the fifth century B.C. Confucius, the Chinese teacher and philosopher whose thought influenced two millennia, understood the effect of music on human character and emotional self-control. He taught that music should be in harmony with Tao, the mandate of heaven, and should follow the alternation of yin and yang—the heavy and light beats whose pulsing rhythm governs the cosmos. In the following century Plato, the Athenian thinker who helped lay the foundations of European culture, was teaching that the sense of rhythm and melody has been implanted in us by the gods and is meant to be developed in imitation of the motion of the heavenly bodies. Plato heard "the music of the spheres" and found there a model for a well-ordered and virtuous human society. The theory of the harmony of celestial spheres was revived in later centuries by Augustine, Boethius, Kepler, Descartes, Leibnitz. Without trying to revive such theories in our own time, we can share their intuitions as we listen for the song of life that each of us is invited to discover, to appreciate, and to move with harmoniously.

How do I listen to this universal song of life? Listening, I have come to understand, is a matter of openness. Catching the rhythm of the song of life that rings through the world might mean I have to gently open myself more to the surrounding situation, to other people, and even to my own deepest reality.

Oftentimes in our lives, there are situations and circumstances that we do not like but are powerless to change. These circumstances may be the result of the general political or economic condition of the country, our job or lack of job, a disabling accident or illness. In place of harmony there is tension and anxiety in our life. If we cannot change our situation, perhaps we can change our evaluation of it by listening to the broader context or placing it in the greater timespan. Perhaps only then will we begin to hear other, more positive sides of the situation that we missed at first. In the total song of life the dissonant, cacophonous elements have to be accepted, transcended, and absorbed into the dominant melody.

In the course of a conversation with someone I do not yet know very well, an openness to every nuance and inflection of his or her voice may enable me to hear the song of that person's life. If I am to be helpful in the situation, I will pay attention to nonverbal cues as much as to the actual topics of our conversation. The most important things may not get mentioned at all because they are too painful or too mysterious to be put into words. The listener's openness may detect the inaudible words and respond on that deep level in harmony with the speaker's unexpressed song of woundedness or bewilderment or joy.

I need to listen also to the song that is me, to my aspirations and failings, my inner harmonies and disharmonies. Today there is a technology for listening to one's own biorhythms, and this scientific approach may be helpful to certain individuals. But it is possible to monitor myself without any machinery if I know my own levels of tolerance. I cannot expect the same performance from myself at all times, as if I were a computerized robot. There are times of the day, times of the month, times of my life cycle when I know that I am likely to feel lazy or touchy or unreasonable, and other times when I am usually optimistic and outgoing. When I am in tune with my own rhythms I can accept more easily the gifted but limited reality that I am, the song of my own life.

Music Without a Sound

The song that I am resonates in the open space at the center of my being. We have already observed how this central openness is characteristic of the human person and is the root of the ability to hear. I am not the source of the song that resounds in my inmost being. I am not the singer but the listener to that song. At my inmost center I am the recipient, not the giver. My ultimate openness is not the openness with which I listen to my life situation or my fellow human beings or my own biorhythms, but my openness to the creating God from whom I receive the totality of my being as a gift. God is the source of the song that I am. God is my music. And God is the music that sounds in all people, events, and things when I listen to them with full openness. All creatures sing something about the mystery or the beauty of their creator. Even when I cannot put words to the song of life, I can hear an affirmation of a saving, sustaining, divine presence.

In a poem called "The Spiritual Canticle" describing the relationship of intimacy with God, St. John of the Cross described his Beloved in a paradoxical metaphor. God, he wrote, is "music without a sound, sonorous solitude." In his commentary on the poem, John attempted to explain the paradox by pointing out that the divine music can best be heard in solitude and silence. The sonorous music is not a physical sound that vibrates the eardrum but something transcending the senses. Physical solitude and silence remove the distracting noises that prevent us from hearing on deeper levels. John of the Cross was a strong advocate of disciplining or "emptying" the external senses as well as the memory, intellect, and will, so as to open other levels of sensitivity within the self.

"Openness to the divine music that is heard without a sound" provides an elaborate description of the experience of praying. In simpler terms, prayer is listening. I pray when I turn a listening ear and a listening heart towards God. Perhaps most of the time I hear nothing, but I pray by being content to wait in the silence and to offer the prayer of my yearning, aching openness. The God I listen for is a speaking God, but the ways he speaks may be so unexpected, subtle, quiet, or surprising that I fail to recognize them for what they are. I may be expecting God to speak in a song of thundering majesty and then miss the song that he is whispering in a gentle breeze or in the smile of a friend, or in a negative experience such as a stab of arthritic pain or the loss of a loved one.

When God speaks, not many words are needed. A single word is enough to create the world and to recreate it. A single word, the sound of my name, is enough to awaken, affirm, and energize me to the depths of my being. A story from the eighteenth-century Jewish Hasidic tradition related by Martin Buber communicates something of the power of the divine word. It was the custom to begin the scripture reading with the phrase, "And God said" or "And God spoke, saying." But whenever Rabbi Zusya heard that introductory phrase, he was overcome with emotion and could not control his reactions. He had to be taken out into the hallway or to the woodshed where he pounded the walls and repeatedly cried out the words "And God spoke! And God spoke!" By the time Rabbi Zusya had calmed down, the reading and instruction were over. He missed hearing the message because of his sensitivity, but he was fully open to the transforming power of the word.

Hearing the Word in the Old Testament

The people who wrote the books of both the Old and New Testaments belonged to what communications theorist Marshall McLuhan called an ear culture, as distinct from a literary or eye-oriented culture. Theirs was a religion of the proclaimed word, a religion of hearing the word of the Lord. The categories in which they thought were predominantly auditory and were associated with events and activities. Their God was a speaking and acting God who demanded service, obedience, and fidelity. For the Hebrew people, hearing meant feeling and doing something; words were to be acted upon, not merely written down. The word of God was a cohesive force that held the people together. If a single individual failed to heed and keep the word of God, there were unfortunate consequences for the whole community. Conversely, one person's attentiveness to God's word might bring blessings on the whole community. The prophets in Israel were expected to devote themselves attentively to the revealed divine word and communicate its message to others.

The Israelites also desired their prophets to serve as a buffer between themselves and the unsheathed word of the Lord. In an ear culture, the word of God is endowed with absolute power; to hear it is to risk death. When God spoke from the midst of thunder and lightning on Mount Sinai, the people trembled with fear. For safety's sake, they thrust Moses forward and instructed him to mediate God's word to them. They reasoned as follows:

> We have heard his voice from the midst of the fire and have found out today that a man can still live after God has spoken with him. But why should we die now? Surely this great fire will consume us. If we hear the voice of the Lord, our God, any more, we shall die. . . . Go closer, you, and hear all that the Lord, our God, will say, and then tell us what the Lord, our God, tells you; we will listen and obey. [Deut. 5:24–26]

Moses became the prophet without equal because he was privileged to hear and speak with God face to face, "as one man speaks to another" [Exod. 33:11].

Centuries after Moses, another great prophet was called up to preside over the origins of the monarchy in Israel. The calling of the prophet Samuel is particularly instructive for an understanding of hearing in the Old Testament. Samuel had been raised from childhood in the temple of the Lord at Shiloh. The chief priest of the temple, Eli, was devout but no longer willing or able, in his old age, to discipline his unruly sons and stop them from victimizing the pilgrims who came to worship in the temple. In this situation of laxity and injustice, Samuel managed to maintain his childhood innocence, simplicity, and openness. The Lord is accustomed to reveal his word to people such as Samuel because they are able to hear what the clever and the learned are usually unable to hear. In the lifetime of Eli, "a revelation of the Lord was uncommon and vision infrequent" [1 Sam. 3:7].

One of the duties assigned to the young Samuel was to keep the lamp burning in the temple where the ark of God was. At night he slept there, by the lamp and the ark. One night the Lord called Samuel by name. The youth was startled awake, but his first reaction was to say, "Here I am," as he got to his feet and ran to Eli, who slept in a place nearby. But it was not Eli who had called, so Samuel went back to bed, perhaps thinking he had been having a vivid dream. "Again the Lord called Samuel, who rose and went to Eli. 'Here I am,' he said, 'You called me.' But he answered, 'I did not call you, my son. Go back to sleep" [1 Sam. 3:6]. Then the same thing happened a third time, and the Bible repeats the incident in identical language. But by the third time, Eli understood what was happening, and he counseled Samuel not to be frightened by this voice in the night but if he should again hear his name called, wait there and answer, "Speak, Lord, for your servant is listening." The reader does not know whether the Lord will speak a fourth time, nor did Samuel know. But as soon as Samuel was asleep, the Lord called out as before, "Samuel, Samuel!" and Samuel responded as Eli had directed. Immediately the message came, and it was a terrible judgment on the house of Eli introduced by a metaphor that would have been easily grasped in a tribal, ear culture: "I am about to do something in Israel that will cause the ears of everyone who hears it to ring" [1 Sam. 3:11].

After this initiation into the career of prophet, Samuel became a faithful transmitter of the Lord's messages to his people, "not permitting any word of his to be without effect" [1 Sam. 3:19]. The primary task of his service, as Samuel had learned on that unforgettable night, was to listen: "Speak, Lord for your servant is listening." Servant of the Lord means *listener* first of all. Later, another prophet would underline this meaning in the third song of the Servant of Yahweh: "Morning after morning, he opens my ear that I may hear" [Isa. 50:4].

The phase that follows hearing the word of the Lord is wholehearted obedience. "Ears open to obedience you gave me," says the psalmist [Ps. 40:7]. The Old Testament also records a lengthy history of disobedience, beginning with the journey through the desert. "Oh, that today you would hear his voice: 'Harden not your hearts as at Meribah, as in the day of Messah in the desert'" [Ps. 95:7–8]. To the prophet Ezekiel God complained, "Son of man, you live in the midst of a rebellious house; they have eyes to see but do not see, and ears to hear but do not hear, for they are a rebellious house" [Ezek. 12:2]. Zechariah accused the people of deliberate deafness:

> They refused to listen; they stubbornly turned their backs and stopped their ears so as not to hear. And they made their hearts diamond hard so as not to hear the teaching and the message that the Lord of hosts had sent by his spirit through the former prophets. [Zech. 7:11]

As a result of his people's refusal to listen, God stopped speaking to them. The prophet Amos predicted God's silence: "Yes, days are coming, says the Lord God, when I will send famine upon the land. Not a famine of bread, or thirst for water, but for hearing the word of the Lord" [Amos 8:11]. God hoped to teach his people that they needed his word to live on as they needed bread [Deut. 8:3], and that "it is not the various kinds of fruits that nourish man, but it is your word that preserves those who believe you" [Wisd. of Sol.: 16:26].

During the centuries of God's silence immediately before the New Testament era, the people of God re-read the postexilic prophets as well as the psalms and wisdom books. There they found promises of a coming "day of the Lord" when the word of God would once again be heard in the land. Miracles would herald that day: "Then will the eyes of the blind be opened, the ears of the deaf be cleared; then will the lame leap like a stag, then the tongue of the dumb will sing" [Isa. 35:5–6]. On that day the word will resound so powerfully that the deaf will hear it and the dumb will break into song, a new song, the song of life and salvation.

Hearing the Word in the Gospels

The gospels proclaim that the expected day of the Lord is the day of Jesus Christ. The miracles of Jesus, especially the healing of the deaf, are signs of the messianic day of salvation [see Matt. 11:2–5]. To hear Jesus Christ was salvation and beatitude; it was even life from the dead, for "an hour is coming, has indeed come, when the dead shall hear the voice of the Son of God, and those who have heeded it shall live" [John 5:25]. God himself spoke through his son Jesus: "This is my beloved Son on whom my favor rests. Listen to him" [Matt. 17:5]. Human hearing found its fulfillment in listening to the words of Jesus:

> Blest are your eyes because they see and blest are your ears because they hear. I assure you, many a prophet and many a saint longed to see what you see but did not see it, to hear what you hear but did not hear it. [Matt. 13:16–17]

The Gospel of Mark relates a dramatic cure of a deaf man to underline the importance of openness to the message of Jesus [Mark 7:31–37]. In some ways, the deaf man is symbolic of everyman, and his healing is an example of what Jesus wanted to do for all people: to unloose them from everything that kept them closed in upon themselves and to turn their closure into openness. The man in the gospel story was probably not deaf from birth, for he had once known how to speak, but was now afflicted with a speech impediment concomitant with his deafness. In this condition, the man was brought before Jesus by friends who begged the miracle worker to lay his hand on the deaf man. They had seen Jesus heal by the touch of his hand or by a word of command, and they hoped he could dispatch this case without much ado. But Jesus saw a great significance in the deaf man's silent, self-enclosed life and felt moved to treat him with special attention. As a sign of the importance of what he was going to do, as much as for the sake of privacy, Jesus "took him off by himself away from the crowd" [Mark 7:33]. The healing took place in almost a ceremonial manner. First, Jesus put his fingers into the man's deaf ears. Next he spat on his fingers and touched the man's mute tongue with his saliva.

Then Jesus looked up to heaven as though in supplication, and "emitted a groan" almost as if he were struggling with a powerful resistance [Mark 7:34]. Finally, Jesus gave the deaf man his full attention and spoke a single word of command, "*Ephphatha!* (Be opened!)." The evangelist recorded the original Aramaic form of Jesus' word, perhaps because he wished to draw attention to this injunction about openness. The result was instantaneous: "At once the man's ears were opened; he was freed from the impediment, and began to speak plainly" [Mark 7:35]. The healed man stood before Jesus in total openness and gratefulness. A typical Markan conclusion follows as Jesus attempts to impose secrecy upon the crowd who had witnessed the miracle from a distance, but the delighted people only proclaimed it all the more: "He has done everything well! He makes the deaf hear and the mute speak!" [Mark 7:37, with allusion to Isa. 35:5].

When the newly healed deaf-mute stood before Jesus ready to hear and respond to him wholeheartedly, he was a model of the discipleship Jesus expected from his followers. Again and again Jesus called for openness and obedience, hearing his word and keeping it [see Luke 7:49; 8:21; 10:16; 11:28; 14:35]. He found many, even tax collectors and sinners [Luke 15:1], who were eager to listen to his teaching and his disputes with the scribes and pharisees: "indeed the entire populace was listening to him and hanging on his words" [Luke 19:48]. But those who were prepared to live by his words were few [see John 6:66]. Jesus accused his listeners of having ears but not hearing, because they deliberately closed the ears of their heart and refused to give him that full measure of listening that culminates in willing obedience.

In the fourth gospel, a major theme is the revelation of God's word and its acceptance or rejection. Jesus came as the bearer of a saving truth that he had heard from God [John 8:40]. All who heard his voice, like the people of the Samaritan town of Shechem, and freely decided to become followers of Jesus could hope for a share in his salvation [John 4:42]. Those who were not of God "could not bear" to hear his word [John 8:43 and 47]. The fourth gospel promises a mysterious intercessory power to those who hear and assimilate the words of Jesus so as to live by them: "If you live in me, and my words stay part of you, you may ask what you will—it will be done for you" [John 15:7].

Conclusion

In this first chapter, the ordinary experience of hearing has been our doorway to unsuspected corridors of meaning. On the purely physical level, the ability to hear is a precious human potency that serves us unceasingly, without cost and often without appreciation. Beyond the physical level, hearing connects with our interiority and the wellspring of human judgments, decisions, and actions. Reflection on the deeper symbolism of hearing and of deafness led to insights about our fundamental human openness and our attempted closure when reality seems too threatening. Tracing the theme of hearing through the Bible revealed the important role given in the history of salvation to this ordinary phenomenon. Hearing the word of God and keeping it are cornerstones of biblical religion.

The mystery hidden in the ordinary experience of hearing may be perceived as a song of life. There is a strand of texts in the Bible that suggest we may always find the melody of song if we listen intently enough to the word God speaks in our daily life, even when his word seems harsh in our ears at first. The psalmists were full of the melody of this song, which they called "a new song": "Sing to the Lord a new song of praise in the assembly of the faithful" [Ps. 149:1]. Their new song was repeated with variations in half a dozen psalms. The word "psalm" already implies a song of praise with some instrumental accompaniment, a religious song blessing the name of God and announcing his saving acts in history [see Ps. 144:9 or 33:3]. The poets of the Hebrew psalter were also attuned to the rhythms God had placed in creation: wind, fire, rain, soil, the sea and sky; birds, beasts, and growing things; the movements of all that lived and died on the face of the earth [Ps. 68:8–11; 104:1–35]. The prophet Isaiah, in an image that is almost entirely auditory, described the faithful Yahwist marching through life to the tune of song, lyre, and flute:

> You will sing as on a night when a feast is observed, and be merry of heart, as one marching along with a flute toward the mountain of the Lord, toward the rock of Israel accompanied by the timbrels and lyres. [Isa. 30:29]

The destination of this marcher is Mount Zion, the city of God. The New Testament devotes a large portion of its concluding book to a description of the heavenly Jerusalem, the final goal of all who hear the word of God and keep it. St. Paul was content to say that "Eye has not seen, ear has not heard, nor has it so much as dawned on man what God has prepared for those who love him" [1 Cor. 2:9, alluding to Isa. 64:3]. But the Apocalypse, or Book of Revelation, attempted to supply tantalizing details of life in the new, heavenly Jerusalem. The symbolism used is heavily auditory: angelic voices, new songs, the melody of harpists, trumpets, and incessant acclamations of praise. In stark contrast, the kingdom of evil is depicted as a place of eerie silence, devoid of the sounds of ordinary life and happiness:

> No tunes of harpists and minstrels, of flutists and trumpeters, shall ever again be heard in you. . . . No sound of the millstone shall ever again be heard in you. . . . No voices of bride and groom shall ever again be heard in you. [Rev. 18:22–23]

But the obedient disciples of Jesus who prove victorious over evil shall have a place in the city of God, where they will sing a "new song" in the liturgy that glorifies the One who sits upon the throne [Rev. 5:9–10; 14:2; 15:2–4]. The song of life that they had listened for on earth will become the new song that they delight to repeat forever. Hearing and response will have only one objective then: to listen to the word of the Spirit and the Bride, and to answer from the heart. "The Spirit and the Bride say, 'Come!' Let him who *hears* answer, 'Come!'" [Rev. 22:17; see also the promise in John 14:23]. The ordinary experience of hearing unfolds in a mystery of welcoming openness and surrender.

SOURCES

Bromiley, Geoffrey W., ed. *Theological Dictionary of the New Testament,* s.v. "Akouo." Grand Rapids: Eerdmans, 1964.

Buber, Martin. *Tales of the Hasidim: The Early Masters.* New York: Schocken Books, 1947.

Encyclopaedia Britannica, 15th ed., Macropaedia, s.v. "Music, Art of "; "Musical Rhythm"; "Music Theory"; "Sound."

Keller, Helen. *The Story of My Life.* New York: Dell, 1961.

Léon-Dufour, Xavier, ed. *Dictionary of Biblical Theology,* 2d rev. ed., s.v. "Listen." New York: Seabury Press, 1973.

McLuhan, Marshall, *Understanding Media.* New York: Signet Books, 1964.

Taffet, David. "Music, Mysticism and Bifrost: The Rainbow Bridge." *Studia Mystica* III, no. 2 (Summer 1980).

2 Seeing

. . . .

Detecting the mystery hidden in ordinary things and ordinary experiences may often be done by honing one's faculty of vision. Teilhard de Chardin is sometimes quoted, from *The Divine Milieu:* "Nothing is profane for the one who knows how to see." Seeing the mysterious, sacral dimensions of reality is partly an art to be learned and partly a gift. Everything we learn about seeing will be directly helpful to the objective of this book, which is to open new vistas into the ordinary. Seeing, like hearing, is itself one of the ordinary human experiences that conceal mystery upon mystery. Reflecting on seeing in this chapter, we hope to enlarge our vision as we discover more about this remarkable power.

I rarely have a purely *visual* experience. Even when I am gazing at a painting in an art gallery and my predominant sensation is visual, still my other senses are picking up ambient information from the room or the painting itself, and my brain is synthesizing and recording a total perception. Perception is intersensory, as each sense receiver contributes its input to the final image that comes to my attention. Yet the major part of what I know about the world I live in comes through my eyes. Eyesight is generally considered the most valuable of the senses. The desire to see whatever can be seen has moved scientific technology to extend eyesight millions of light years by means of the telescope, and to penetrate the infinitesimal by means of the electron microscope. Seeing, like hearing, points to an underlying openness to all that is, but more in the mode of an observer than a participant, more like one observing a football game from the grandstand than one playing on the field.

The human eye is dependent on direct or reflected light in

order to function, but is sensitive to only about thirty percent of the electromagnetic spectrum. Wavelengths outside our range might show details or colors that are imperceptible to our unaided eyes. Even within our range of vision, not everything that stimulates the nerve fibers of our eyes is actually perceived as a visual image. Some stimuli are canceled out before they reach the vision control area of the brain, and others are discarded in the brain's process of synthesizing a recognizable visual image. Everything suggests that there is more to be noted in this world of vision than we are aware of ordinarily.

The Marvel of Eyesight

The tiny, one-celled amoeba is all eye, in the sense that it lacks a specialized eyespot and is sensitive to light anywhere on its surface. In contrast, the human eye is a highly specialized organ with millions of light-sensitive neural cells—rods and cones—in its retina. Incoming light waves are focused by the pliable lens to fall on the retina, which is an extension of the brain via the optic nerve. Like the image projected on film by a camera lens, the image that falls on the retina of the eye is upside down and needs to be reversed in the interpretive processing it receives in the brain. Like the camera image also, the retinal image is two-dimensional and needs to be given a depth dimension by brain processes that combine images from both eyes and utilize other data as well.

The retinal rods and cones are the light receptors of the eye. The cones, about seven million in number, are concentrated in an area called the fovea and are specialized to absorb either blue or green or yellow. Working in combination, the cone cells give us sharp, daylight, color vision. Under controlled conditions, about 130 gradations in color can be distinguished, as well as shadings within a given color. Vision in dim light or darkness is accomplished by the rods, which are ten to twenty times more numerous than the cones. Cones are not renewable, but rod segments are constantly sloughed and regenerated every week of our lives.

If we were to follow the path of a single particle or photon of light energy on its journey through the lens of the eye to the retina, we would find that it is first absorbed by a single molecule of visual pigment called rhodopsin in a rod cell, and then ceases to be light because it has been absorbed by matter. The rhodopsin molecule, momentarily illuminated and energized, splits into its component chemical and protein substance, which will be recombined again in the subsequent darkness. The process of splitting releases positively charged atoms, leaving behind negatively charged atoms and causing a difference in electrical potential that can be transmitted along a nerve fiber to the brain. The light energy of the photon has become a neural impulse that can be used by the brain in its synthesis of the total visual image corresponding to the object of our gaze. The transformation from one form of energy to another has been accomplished by the mini-explosion or firing of a rhodopsin molecule. This process goes on simultaneously in millions of rods and cones in a repeated sequence of illumination and darkness, discharge and recharge.

Our eyes, at least during waking hours, are in almost continual motion, sweeping back and forth, up and down to pick out patterns and shapes in our perceptual field. It has been shown by sensitive instruments that, even when we gaze steadily and intently at a single object, our eyes are never still for longer than a fraction of a second. If the eye held the object any longer, the retina would adapt to the stimulus and the image would disappear. Instead of holding the object in view, the eye continually lets it go and returns to it so that a fresh stimulus may fall on the rods and cones. The movement happens so rapidly, and the brain is so efficient at filling in the gaps, that we do not notice what is actually happening.

In more ways than one, we do not notice what is actually happening when we look at an object. This description of the function of eyesight indicates the complexity of the visual process and the coordination of eye and brain that is involved. If vision did not come naturally, most of us would never master it!

A World to Observe

Through our senses, we interact with the world around us and with the persons, events, and objects that fill our ordinary daily experience. Since eyesight is the dominant way most people relate to the world, what we have learned about the process of vision may reveal an important truth about the inter-relation of people with their environment. Reflection on hearing has revealed the fundamental human dimension of openness to the world, and we have already noted that eyesight partakes of this openness in the manner of an observer.

An observer does not immediately intend to do anything but observe. An observer prefers not to interfere or to control a situation, but to respond and participate in it by observation. An observer's preferred mode of action is to let things be as they are rather than to manipulate or rearrange them in any other way. The more accurately and completely the observer can appreciate circumstances as they are, the better he or she is as observer. Impartiality and objectivity seem characteristic of good observers.

Facts we have learned about the function of the eye confirm its role as observer of the world. The eye records what is there as accurately as a camera or a mirror, leaving the object untouched, undamaged. The eye is not a hand that reaches out and grasps, but only a receiver that accepts whatever is present to it. The eye operates not by conquest but by regard or respect. The eye cannot look directly at itself because its object must always be separate and away. Eyesight preserves a certain distance from its object for the sake of observing it. We recall also that the eye cannot hold objects in its gaze for very long, but needs a new stimulus every few microseconds of observation.

In my relationships with the people, things, and events of my daily life, I can grasp, hold, and manipulate for my own purposes, or I can let go, let be, and observe respectfully. Both modes of relating to the world can be appropriate, depending on the situation. For example, if I want to prepare a meal, I will have to do more than look at the potatoes with an admiring, respecting gaze; I will have to take them in hand and peel them for cooking. Nature has endowed me with hands as well as eyes. But if the only or the predominant way I relate to reality is by attempting to manipulate and control, then I am neglecting a major sector of my humanness as revealed in the observer function of my most important sensory power, eyesight. The mode of functioning natural to my eyesight suggests that I not attempt to dominate everything and everyone I encounter, but should appreciate people, things, and events as they are in their own right. My natural visual processes suggest that, instead of a grasping approach to the world, I can be content with letting objects be themselves, affirming their right to be and to become what they are meant to be.

Learning to be present to the other as a gentle, respectful observer seems culturally more difficult for Westerners than for people from traditional oriental cultures. The contemporary Korean artist Kyu-Baik Hwang, working in the style known as "magic realism," has produced mezzotints of an ordinary hillside of soft, spring grass meticulously depicted as he observed it. To take an example from another medium, Zen Buddhist scholar D. S. Suzuki has drawn attention to a haiku poem by the eighteenth-century Japanese master, Basho:

> When closely inspected,
> One notices a nazuna in bloom
> Under the hedge.

The nazuna has a flower so tiny it goes unappreciated by all but the closest observers. A contrasting Western response to a similar situation is recorded in the poem "Flower in the Crannied Wall" by the nineteenth-century Englishman Alfred Tennyson, who plucked the flower from its cranny and held it in his hand as he mused on its beauty. Basho was content to observe the nazuna in its natural position under the hedge, respectful of its own life and uniqueness. Tennyson wrote his poem about a plucked flower that had already begun to lose the fullness of its being and would eventually wither in his hand.

The mysteries concealed in ordinary realities are often revealed most fully to the eye that observes rather than to the hand that seizes and holds. The grasp closes on the exterior surface of the object, while the respectful gaze may sometimes catch a glimpse of mysteries within. Reality can be luminous and radiant with inner meaning for eyes that are content to observe with gentleness and respect.

To Look and to See

There is a distinction between looking and seeing, and these terms will be used in their strict connotation throughout this chapter. I look with my eyes, but it is my whole self who sees. What I can see goes far beyond what my eyes look upon. Seeing usually has its beginning in looking; but there is more to be seen than meets the looking eye. The "more than" is what I see when I go beyond mere looking. To look requires normal eyesight and brain functioning; to see requires insight. Not everyone who looks can see or wants to see. Many are satisfied with simply looking, but those who would like to penetrate the mysterious depths of ordinary realities must learn to see. Looking relates to reality by classifying, recognizing, naming, analyzing, holding, appropriating, utilizing, controlling. Seeing relates to reality more in the patient, receptive, gentle observer mode that we have just studied.

The idioms of ordinary speech sometimes reflect this distinction between looking and seeing. When something is directly in front of me but not figural in my perception, I may say, "I can't see for looking." I may tell someone, "I have to see the abbot after supper," meaning that I want to discuss something with the abbot, not merely look at him. Likewise, we use the expressions "I see what you mean," "I can see right through that excuse," "See that you return it afterwards." In such expressions the word "look" would be inappropriate, because the reference is not to physical eyesight. In other common idioms the word "look" fits perfectly, and "see" would be inappropriate: "Look before you leap," "Look out for falling rock," "Look in the bottom drawer," "Wow, look at that!" "Look me in the eye and say that."

When I look at an object, say my alarm clock, I perceive the

face of it, the side turned towards me; but I *see* the whole clock
with a certain thickness and a back. I look at the face alone, but
see more than the face. Everything in reality has a "more than,"
another side that I must see if I am to perceive the object in its
totality. When I look I perceive initially only the superficial
aspect or appearance of the object. The shift from looking at a
part or several parts to seeing the whole is a major step in the
art of seeing.

The shift to a holistic view is relatively easy when the object
is something like an alarm clock, but not so easy when it comes
to events that happen in my life, and even more difficult when
I am confronting other people. The sweeping look I direct
towards the person speaking to me often takes in only the out-
ward appearance: style of hair, color of eyes, facial features and
expression, animation or lack of animation, half smile or half
frown, gestures attempted then discontinued—all the cues that
might indicate the person's intentions or feelings towards me. I
have looked the person over but may never see the full reality
of this human being, because I overlooked him or her as person. How difficult to *see* people as they are precisely as human
beings, with the beauty of ideals and aspirations, the dignity of
a long, inner quest, the complexity of a life history, the fidelity
and failings of the past, the uniqueness of talents and abilities.
How difficult to see the invisible within the visible form before
me!

Seeing does not artificially manufacture what it sees, but
perceives the reality always already present in the object, as a
prism diffracts white light into a spectrum of color really
present in the white, or as water droplets in the air separate
sunlight into the familiar bands of the rainbow. Seeing sees reality as it is, beneath and beyond the surface. Not that what we
look at is not also real. The face of the alarm clock is as real as
the back, and neither the face alone nor the back alone is the
totality of the clock's reality. If I were to see the springs and
gears inside the clock, I would see still more of its reality. If I
also saw the maker of the clock, I would have a deeper vision
yet. And if I could somehow see all the events whose moments

had been measured by the ticking of this clock, I would perhaps begin to see something of the mystery of this perfectly ordinary clock. That would be but the beginning.

People Who See

I learn to see by opening myself repeatedly, wonderingly, to fresh aspects of the inexhaustible reality before me. An attitude of relaxed, receptive, contemplative attention is helpful, because I will see only as much and as clearly as I want to see. Because I never know what I shall see, there is risk in shifting from looking to seeing; it often seems safer to be satisfied with a quick look that is enough to attach a familiar name to the object and reassure me that I am on customary ground in a manageable world. But safety, security, and the look intent on one limited aspect can mean a life of boredom and drabness. It is people who know how to see who are the most enlivened, enriched, expansive, creative human beings.

A parable recounted by Evelyn Underhill in her book *Practical Mysticism* illustrates the difference between people who see and people who only look. To paraphrase the story, two people are walking the same road on their journey through life. The one who looks is intent on completing his walk as efficiently, comfortably, and economically as he can. He trudges steadily along, eyes fixed on the path in front of him, unconcerned about what may lie on either side or about the fine quality of the day. The person with a developed capacity for seeing travels the same path but discovers new wonders at every step: the exhilarating sunlight, the refreshing breeze, the magic presences that salute him from hidden fields. His journey is sometimes laborious but always enthralling and highly meaningful. At the end of the journey the two travelers compare notes. The one who merely looked cannot believe that the traveler who saw so much was truly on the same road. Underhill concludes that the only proof would be to persuade the one who only looked to go and see for himself.

Some of us have lost our capacity for seeing, or allowed it to atrophy with disuse, but it may be possible to recover this gift, which is also an art that can be developed with practice. Associating with people who see can provide a strong incentive. If we are not blessed with the living companionship of such people, we can meet many masters of seeing in the creative works of art and literature that they have left to the world. The following sections will dwell on select examples of people who see.

To see as a child.   Many children go through periods of "seeing" as distinct from merely looking. At such times they can become absorbed in an object they have never encountered before, can amuse themselves for hours with the simplest things, can delight in having things repeated again and again. I learned something about seeing through a child's eyes from my five-year-old niece Jessica, when she came for a visit to the monastery with her family. One morning we all piled into the van for a picnic lunch at Causey Reservoir. On approaching the picnic site my first thought was to set things up for the meal, unload the boxes of hotdogs and potato chips, choose a table in the shade, and build a fire so that we could all enjoy the picnic. When the van came to a stop Jessica and I were the first ones out. She immediately began to explore and had not gone very far when she stopped and exclaimed with delight. I paused in my tasks long enough to glance in her direction and observe her picking up a feather from the side of the road. She brought it to me with the pride of one exhibiting a valuable treasure instead of an old feather dropped from a molting hawk. I murmured, "That's very nice, Jessica. Do you want to help me unload the van?" Later, when I reflected on this incident, I realized that Jessica saw far more in that feather than I could or was willing to see at that moment. As she turned the feather over in her little hands and examined its markings, what could the eyes of her imagination perceive? Perhaps she saw a large bird circling proudly in the blue sky, the ripple being made by this feather in the wind as the bird flew, the feeling of loss as the feather worked loose from the wing, its long erratic glide to the ground where it finally came to rest beside the road. I had merely looked at the feather, recognized it as coming from a hawk's wing, and proceeded with my efficient preparations for the picnic. Jessica had begun having a picnic as soon as the van door opened and she found the feather; this was a feast already prepared for her in a world that she still found exciting and new. She saw the feather as it deserved to be seen and was enriched by her experience; I merely looked and then went back to my preoccupations.

Prophets and poets.   The prophets of the Old Testament were originally called "seers," as we learn from a remark in one of the historical books: "He who is now called prophet was formerly called seer" [1 Sam. 9:9]. The first and greatest of these seers was the prophet Moses. In the episode of the calling of Moses on Mount Horeb in the Sinai desert, the visual object that is central in the account is a burning bush. Moses was tending his father-in-law's flock in the desert when the Lord appeared to him in what looked like fire flaming from an ordinary bush. "As Moses *looked on,* he was surprised to *see* that the bush, though on fire, was not consumed" [Exod. 3:2, italics added]. Looking was followed by seeing, and Moses decided to take a closer look in order the better to see this wonder. "When the Lord saw him coming over to look at it more closely, God called out to him from the bush, 'Moses! Moses!' He answered, 'Here I am.' God said, 'Come no nearer! Remove the sandals from your feet, for the place where you stand is holy ground" [Exod. 3:4–5]. The burning bush is mentioned no more, and the encounter becomes principally an auditory one as the invisible God summons and commissions his prophet. For our interests, the point to be noted is that if Moses had been content with a cursory look and had dismissed the burning bush as a desert mirage, he might never have become God's seer.

Poets and creative authors keep alive in the culture the art of seeing the dimension of mystery and beauty in life. For one who can see, there can be a burning bush experience with the most ordinary and commonplace realities of life such as the cedar tree growing in the back yard. Such a seer is the contemporary author, Annie Dillard, who has described an experience she had as a *Pilgrim at Tinker Creek* when a familiar tree seemed to be transfigured before her eyes and the grass she stood on mirrored the vision. Dillard stressed that she was simply observing and not thinking of anything at all when she saw the "tree with lights in it." She described what she saw: "I saw the backyard cedar where the mourning doves roost charged and transfigured, each cell buzzing with flame. I stood on the grass with the lights in it, grass that was wholly fire, utterly focused and utterly dreamed." Gradually "the cells unflamed" and Dillard was looking once more at her familiar back yard. But she is never likely to forget that the most familiar objects conceal a depth of being that borders on the sacred.

Near the abrupt end of his long monastic life, Thomas Merton had an experience of seeing that jerked him out of his habitual manner of looking at things and left him with a sense of reality illuminated and transparent. The experience is described in *The Asian Journal of Thomas Merton,* and took place on the island of Sri Lanka, at Polonnaruwa, where there are giant stone statues of Buddha, Ananda, and others. Merton went there with his camera as a typical tourist, but he also removed his shoes and approached the figures as a pilgrim. He gazed intently and respectfully at these huge carved images with folded arms and half smiles, and the figures gazed back at Merton. The experience, as he described it in his journal, was overpowering: "Looking at these figures I was suddenly, almost forcibly jerked clean out of the habitual, half-tied vision of things, and an inner clearness, clarity, as if exploding from the rocks themselves, became evident and obvious." The "habitual, half-tied" tourist's look at curious objects shifted suddenly and almost forcibly to an insight of clarity, evidence, and validity that seemed to explode free from the rock itself. The tourist Merton was liberated to become completely the pilgrim who had now reached the climax of his pilgrimage to Asia.

Artists.   Artists are seers who have the added gift of enabling others to see their vision. Their creative works remain after them so that others may look and see as the original artists saw. A single example will have to represent this vast field of art. I have selected the nineteenth-century Dutch painter Vincent van Gogh, whose greatness was not appreciated until long after his suicide at the age of thirty-seven. During his lifetime, he sold only two paintings; today a single one of his oils has brought over five million dollars on auction.

Vincent, to use the name with which he signed his works, wanted at first to become a minister to bring the consolation of

religion to the very poor. He failed as a minister and broke all
ties with organized religion, but turned to art in the last decade
of his short life as perhaps a better medium through which to
bring meaning and beauty to people and open their eyes to the
deeper mysteries of life. Vincent remained attracted to ordinary
things like houses, ships, cafés, flower vases; to common scenes
of nature, cypresses, and sunflowers; to simple people such as
peasants working or eating potatoes, shopkeepers, weavers,
postmen, prostitutes. In the faces of common people, seasoned
by life's trials and joys, Vincent could see the sacred; and he
wanted to symbolize that quality by the radiance and vibration
of his paints rather than by halos. Vincent became a colorist in
the final, most productive period of his life, after he moved to
the sunny regions of southern France. For him color was a
means of helping the viewer see more than a color camera could
reproduce in a photograph; color, even when used somewhat
arbitrarily, was intended to awaken the viewer's insight.

Vincent admitted his admiration for Japanese artists whose
work he had studied in Paris. He desired to achieve the clarity
and simplicity they expressed in a few short strokes of the
brush. As Vincent understood the Japanese approach to painting, it began with the prolonged study of a commonplace object such as a blade of grass. When an artist could see and paint
all that could be seen in a blade of grass, he had acquired a
vision of nature that could then be expanded to include all
plants, landscapes, the seasons, animals, and human figures.
Vincent trusted this method, as he wrote to his brother Theo:
"It is looking at things for a long time that ripens you and gives
you a deeper understanding."

One work in which Vincent put the Japanese style to good
use was a large painting of his own familiar bedroom. *The Bedroom at Arles* shows undistinguished furniture, a towel and
clothes hanging from hooks, a mirror and pictures on the walls,
a casement window opening into the room. There are no shadows, and the coloring is "in free flat tones like Japanese prints,"
as he described it to Theo. The colors, predominantly green
with shades of brown and faded blue, are meant to be sugges-
tive of repose. "In a word," wrote Vincent, "to look at the

picture ought to rest the brain or rather the imagination." The viewer sees what Vincent saw in his own bedroom when he looks at the picture and finds it restful.

Unfortunately, there were more stresses in Vincent's life than could be calmed by a good night's rest, and it was not long after completing this work that Vincent suffered a nervous breakdown of some sort and was hospitalized. When he was released the following year and was going through some of his paintings, he judged *The Bedroom* to be the finest, as we learn from another letter to Theo. Vincent at his best was a person who could see the profound mysteries of the ordinary, an artist of intense and tender feeling. Yet he is a tragic figure because he could not see a deeper meaning and purpose in his own afflictions. A person passionately in love with the sun, Vincent lived in intolerable darkness about his own worth as a human being.

Fearing Darkness

Vincent van Gogh experienced the darkness of self-doubt and despair to an extreme degree; but the fear of physical darkness may be an experience many of us can identify with more readily. Although people are not born with a fear of the dark, many children go through a phase of being afraid to sleep in a dark room. At night the familiar, restful bedroom may seem strangely alien and the child cannot be oriented and reassured by reference to familiar objects. Eerie forms materialize out of the shadows; normal sounds become suspicious. Is there another living presence in this room, the child wonders? Best not to take chances by leaving a foot or hand exposed outside the blanket. The blanket seems to provide a cocoon of security against the dark unknown.

Why is it that physical darkness arouses fear, not only in some children but even in some adults? Could there be in our collective unconscious a residue of the primordial fear felt by primitive people who could not, as we can, transform darkness into day by flipping a light switch? Or does the darkness touch off a feeling of alarm much closer to the surface, the fear of blindness and all that blindness entails?

In the dark I half expect danger; my instinct is to anticipate the worst. I feel powerless and vulnerable against forces I cannot see. I may feel an urge to flee but have no sense of direction in the dark. Where I am feels unsafe, but I attempt to bring my apprehension under control and not let it mushroom into panic. I endure the darkness like a pall. This fear of darkness is akin to the fear of being blind.

Blindness

As a sighted person I have difficulty projecting myself into the experience of the permanently blind, difficulty seeing the world that appears to their sightless eyes. In America, about two hundred of every 100,000 people are blind; the rate may be twenty times that in countries with poor health standards. Causes of blindness are extremely variable, and certain causes are avoidable with proper care. Sometimes blindness can be cured. People born blind from cataracts have recovered their vision after surgery; such people, as they adjust to the world's brightness, have learned new meanings of the word "beautiful." Those who have regained their eyesight are likely to become seers rather than mere onlookers, because they will never take their power of vision for granted; merely looking would be like being blind again.

The phenomenon of color blindness affects a number of people without usually diminishing their ability to function. They see colors as identical where most people would detect a difference. Those who know of their color blindness can often distinguish the colors by paying attention to brightness.

All sighted people have a blind area on their retinas where the optic nerve joins the eyeball and there are no rods and cones to receive the incoming light. The blind area is imperceptible by us, because the brain automatically fills in the complete form of the visual object.

Reflecting on the fact that even the sighted have blind spots, and some are color blind, perhaps the experience of blindness is not so foreign to me as I first thought. In fact, it is perhaps worse to be blind in particular areas without knowing it than to know one is totally blind. What are my blind spots, my areas of prejudice where I cannot see any opinion but my own? Have I allowed past experiences to blind or color my view of this or that person so that I can never see them as different from what they once were? In dealing with people of other cultures and races, am I blind to our common humanity so that I see only what differentiates and not what unites us?

The normal eye takes in all that lies within the field of vision, and the brain automatically registers it. Under conditions of severe emotional stress, the brain may bracket out part of the reality that the eyes take in. But normal individuals also have an ability for selective perception of reality, which is a form of willful blindness. They look but do not see. Genuine seeing tends to be more universal. One who sees casts a benevolent eye over the world, accepting and affirming reality as it is. Seeing embraces the ugly as well as the beautiful, the bad as well as the good, the unlovable and the lovable, the painful and the joyful. Seeing is judgment-free. Defectiveness is part of reality and to bracket it from one's seeing is to prefer to be blind. Seeing the ugly side of life does not necessarily mean dwelling on it, but acknowledging its existence and sometimes accepting responsibility for having caused or not prevented it.

Hardest to see and accept responsibility for is the depravity in one's own heart. In the words of Jesus, "From the mind stem evil designs—murder, adulterous conduct, fornication, stealing, false witness, blasphemy. These are the things that make a man impure" [Matt. 15:19–20]. The dark, shadowy side of our character is more visible to those we live with than it is to ourselves. People who have seen their own inner wounds and miseries have sometimes compared the experience to darkness, the dark night of bewilderment and aloneness. Usually it is only when we are able to see God's unconditional love for us that we are also able to see the unlovable side of ourselves; otherwise the sight of our wretchedness could be crushing and demoralizing. In many ways we are blind until the light of God gleams in our face and enables us to see.

"I Am the Light of the World" [John 8:12]

The light that we turn towards in this section is Jesus Christ. He has said, "I came into this world to divide it, to make the sightless see and the seeing blind" [John 9:39]. The restoration of sight to the blind was one of the expected signs of the messianic era, and Jesus frequently healed the blind [Matt. 9:27; Mark 8:22; John 9:1]. Many of the sighted people who witnessed the cures did not see them as signs; they were blind to the true significance. As Jesus said elsewhere, "They look intently as they will but do not see" [Matt. 13:14].

Bartimaeus of Jericho.   One of the most lifelike descriptions of sight restored to the blind is the account in Mark's gospel of the cure of a roadside beggar whose name meant "son of Timaeus" [Mark 10:46]. The incident occurred just prior to Jesus' triumphal entrance into Jerusalem, and may have contributed to the enthusiasm of that entry. A large crowd had already gathered at Jericho to accompany Jesus. Bartimaeus heard the commotion, with the keen sense of hearing developed by many blind people. The man was a spirited and enterprising fellow, not embittered by his handicap. "On hearing that it was Jesus of Nazareth, he began to call out, 'Jesus, Son of David, have pity on me!' " [Mark 10:47]. Bartimaeus must have known Jesus' reputation as a healer, and he did not hesitate to cry out to him with a name guaranteed to draw attention to himself. "Son of David" was a messianic title that would soon be ringing out with Hosannas as Jesus reached Jerusalem. When Bartimaeus used the title, the crowd was initially annoyed and scolded him for his impudence. It was customary anyway to shush importunate beggars, and for them to become all the more importunate. So Bartimaeus "shouted all the louder, 'Son of David, have pity on me' " until Jesus stopped his journey and called the beggar to his side [Mark 10:48]. Bartimaeus jumped to his feet and with a dramatic gesture threw aside the cloak he was using as a blanket. He would not need his beggar's blanket any longer; he was confident that a new life was about to begin for him. The crowd made way for the blind man, who went up to Jesus by following the sound of his voice. Jesus could see the man's condition and his obvious need,

but he wanted to speak with this determined person and hear
what he had to say. "Jesus asked him, 'What do you want me to
do for you?' 'Rabboni,' the blind man said, 'I want to see'"
[Mark 10:51]. His request corresponded to what Jesus wanted of
people throughout his ministry. In Mark's account the cure happened instantaneously, without a touch of Jesus' hand or a word
of command. The blind Bartimaeus could suddenly see the Son
of David standing before him. Jesus told the man he was free to
go: "Your faith has healed you" [Mark 10:52]. The word for
"heal" carries the added note of "save." Bartimaeus started to
follow Jesus up the road toward Jerusalem. The evangelist does
not describe the man's emotions of gratefulness and joy because
the concluding thought was to be a message about discipleship:
only those who have the faith to see can follow Jesus through his
passion and resurrection to eternal salvation.

    Seeing and believing.   The word for "eye" occurs about
a hundred times in the New Testament, a frequency that suggests
the importance of sight in the vocabulary of revelation and salvation. Looking should lead to the seeing that is also believing. But
the eyes may prefer not to see. Jesus said, "If your eyes are good,
your body will be filled with light; if your eyes are bad, your
body will be in darkness" [Matt. 6:22–23]. The eye may content
itself with looking at seductive enticements; Jesus warned: "If
your eye is your downfall, gouge it out and cast it from you!
Better to enter life with one eye than to be thrown with both into
fiery Gehenna" [Matt. 18:9]. Jesus was not ruling out the enjoyment of visually beautiful sights, but he wanted the eye to see
beyond the surface to the ultimate creating and conserving
source. He invited people to "look intently" at the lilies of the
field that are clothed in such splendor, and to remember that God
can provide as well for all human needs [Luke 12:27–28].

    Nowhere do the gospels describe the physical appearance of
Jesus, because their concern is with the faith-vision of Christ as
Lord, savior, and revealer of his Father. Looking at Jesus in his
lifetime was of religious value only if it fostered the seeing that
is faith, described as seeing "the glory of an only Son coming
from the Father" [John 1:14]. After his death and resurrection,
Jesus can be recognized only by faith-seeing. When he ap-

peared, for example, to the disciples on their way to Emmaus,
"their eyes were held, so that they did not recognize him"
[Luke 24:16]. Later, Jesus blessed and broke bread for these disciples in a ritual that was familiar from many meals they had
shared. Then "their eyes were opened up and they recognized
him," but at that moment he vanished from physical view,
leaving them with their faith-vision of him [Luke 24:31]. Ap-
pearing on another occasion, the risen Lord said to Thomas:
"You became a believer because you saw me. Blest are they
who have not seen and have believed" [John 20:29]. In other
texts, the New Testament clearly affirms the independence of
faith from sight [2 Cor. 4:18; 5:7; 1 Pet. 1:8]. Believers are not
to credit rumors that their Lord has appeared publicly, but are
to wait in patient longing for the appointed day of his coming,
when "every eye shall see him, even of those who pierced him"
[Rev. 1:7 and Matt. 24:23–27].

Conclusion

Studying the ordinary experience of vision has disclosed an
expanded horizon of possibilities for seeing. The intricacy of
the eye's function in cooperation with the brain provides the
physical basis for these possibilities. The distinction between
seeing and merely looking was underlined, and examples were
given of people who see the mystery of the ordinary. Finally,
the New Testament data was surveyed, and particularly the link
between seeing and believing.

Are there any limits to seeing? If so, there are people who
will never rest until they have gazed upon those ultimate limits,
because there is an insatiable human desire to see more than has
been seen so far. There is even a desire to see the Absolute, to
see God. The ancient Greeks, who have been called "a people of
the eye," considered the vision of God to be the goal of their
religious rites and their philosophical contemplation. The
Judaeo-Christian tradition tended to stress hearing, to be suspicious of cultic images, and to avoid the suggestion that the living God can be seen face to face [Exod. 33:18–23]. Because it
was feared that seeing the all-holy God would bring death to

sinful human beings, the direct vision of God was anticipated in another age; in this life God could be seen only in his works [Wisd. of Sol. 13:5; Josh. 24:17].

Jesus brought humanity a much clearer but still indistinct vision of God, for he was the revelation of his Father [John 14:9]. Jesus had experienced the "unapproachable light" where God was said to dwell [1 Tim. 6:16; John 6:46]. But seeing God face to face is still reserved for the future [1 John 3:2]. Then we shall see as we are already seen by "the Son of God whose eyes blaze like fire" [Rev. 2:18].

Still, for those who can see into the mystery of all reality, there is even now some fulfillment of the longing that lovers have to gaze upon the face of their beloved [Ps. 63:2–3]. The reflections in this chapter have suggested ways of seeing people, events, and things in a larger perspective that opens onto the mystery of God. Instead of merely looking at the surface of things, I want to see the invisible divine hand guiding the visible events of my life even when these events are unexpected and unwelcome. I want to sharpen my seeing power to detect God's presence in apparent absence, and to catch a new glimpse of his form in experiences that upset my previous image of him. As a believing Christian I want to see my Lord in the sacrament of his body and blood, in the haunting features of my needy brothers and sisters, and in the fellowship of those who gather together anywhere in his name. "No one has ever yet seen God," says John in his letter to the churches, "yet if we love one another, God dwells in us and his love is brought to perfection in us" [1 John 4:12].

SOURCES

Dillard, Annie. *Pilgrim at Tinker Creek.* New York: Bantam, 1975.

Encyclopaedia Britannica, 15th ed., Macropaedia, s.v. "Eye and Vision, Human"; "Photoreception"; "Space Perception"; "Light."

Friedrich, Gerhard, ed. *Theological Dictionary of the New Testament,* vol. V, s.v. "orao." Grand Rapids; Eerdmans, 1967.

Merton, Thomas. *The Asian Journal of Thomas Merton.* New York: New Directions, 1973.

Roskill, Mark, ed. *The Letters of Vincent van Gogh*. New York: Atheneum, 1974.

Schachtel, Ernest G. *Metamorphosis: On the Development of Affect, Perception, Attention and Memory*. New York: Basic Books, 1959.

Suzuki, D. S. *Mysticism: Christian and Buddhist*. New York: Macmillan Co., 1969.

Underhill, Evelyn. *Practical Mysticism*. New York: Dutton, 1943.

3 Walking

As a nation, Americans today are not people who prefer to walk if they have a choice. Most of us prefer to get there faster, and so we usually hop on or into the nearest means of transportation. Our country is crisscrossed by a multibillion dollar system of interstate freeways to enable us to get there faster. For still speedier travel, there is the jet plane, or even supersonic transport, to whisk us across the country in a matter of hours. The faster the vehicle, the more remote it is from walking the ground on foot.

We tend to view walking as a generally unsatisfactory way of reaching our destination; and so we walk only as a last resort, when we cannot park the car any closer, or when the car breaks down, or when there is a transit strike. If all else fails, we know that we can always walk. The ability to walk is taken for granted and seldom appreciated until accident or illness deprives us of the ability temporarily or permanently. Then we miss what we can no longer do.

Walking, like many commonplace activities that we take for granted, deserves to be recognized and appreciated for what it is in itself and for what it symbolizes in the total picture of human existence. A quick consideration reveals the functional purpose of the act of walking: walking is a means of travel or of exercise or of relaxation. A more attentive consideration will reveal the many meanings of walking as an experience in itself. Walking can be used for many purposes, but walking has its own proper meaning, structure, and symbolic content apart from any purpose we may use it for.

The following sections will consider some of the many dimensions of the experience of walking. My reflections will move from the literal to the more symbolic and metaphorical meanings of walking. Ultimately, I will relate the experience of walking to the dynamics of Christian spiritual living, by showing how scripture and spirituality have described the fundamental relationship of a person to God in terms of walking. To walk before God is a person's greatest dignity and responsibility; to walk with God is a person's supreme fulfillment [see Gen. 17:1]. But let us go one step at a time.

Engineered for Walking

The upright posture and general structure of the human body is ideally adapted for walking. My body was built for dynamic activity, for smooth and graceful motion, and when I walk I am doing what comes naturally and comfortably to my skeletal and muscle systems. The length and shape of my bones; the position of joints at hip, knee, ankle, and toes; the synovial fluid that lubricates the joints; the balanced interplay of muscles —all these structural components assure the flexibility necessary for walking.

Walking is aided, too, by a force that acts on the body from outside, the force of gravity. Walking is quite impossible in the weightlessness of space, because the body does not have the force of gravity to help propel it. In a normal gravity field I can stand upright in perfect balance. As soon as I move my ankle to initiate a step, I tilt myself off balance; gravity begins to pull my torso forward and downward. But at the same time one leg is lifting and swinging forward to provide new support and reestablish my balance. As my center of gravity shifts, dozens of different muscles are automatically coordinated to move me one step in front of where I last stood. Gravity continues to help me if I wish to keep moving. In fact, it is easier and smoother to keep walking than to stop. Once I am in motion, gravity helps me to stay in motion. As I walk I lean forward slightly, and my center of gravity moves steadily ahead, alternating somewhat from side to side as I put down one foot and then the other. The feeling of walking and the appearance to an observer is one of continual, flowing movement.

A smooth and graceful style of walking depends on finding

the right length of stride for my particular pair of legs to move my particular weight at just the right speed. When I have hit my stride, I know it immediately. My movement becomes all but effortless because I am perfectly synchronized with the force of gravity and the grade of the terrain. I could go on and on this way, as long as there are no stones or curbs to stumble over, no sharp turns to make, no hills to climb or descend. These variables in my path would call for an adjustment of my stride, but I would quickly recover my smooth forward pace. When I have found my stride, I can take everything in stride. I am caught up in a rhythm of moving feet and swinging arms that seems to carry me along on its own tide. Some people never discover their natural stride because they are impeded by the poor walking habits they have built up over the years. In some cases, these habits can begin to be changed by deliberately stretching the usual length of step. Another aid may be to increase the rate of speed somewhat. The result will be an increased momentum that lightens the step and reduces muscle effort. But my fastest pace is not necessarily my natural stride. My natural stride is a graceful, springy step just long enough and fast enough to maintain the best balance with the force of gravity. The stride that is right for me will be satisfying and relaxing, never exhausting.

The human body is superbly designed for mobility. Mobility was absolutely necessary for survival in the Stone Age, when food had to be gathered wherever it grew, or stalked wherever it roamed. Stone Age humans were often on the move, never staying very long in one place. They crossed continents in their walking migrations. Walking came easily, naturally, and smoothly for primitive human beings.

Today we live in a civilization far advanced from the Stone Age, but the human body has not evolved that much itself. We are becoming a more and more sedentary civilization, while our bodies were engineered for self-propelled mobility. Many people today exercise their minds more than their bodies. As a result, our bodies lose their tonic healthfulness and tend to become overweight, to develop poor circulation, varicose veins, hardening of the arteries, and assorted aches and pains.

The answer is not to return to a Stone Age culture, but to rediscover our own two feet. We need to discover ourselves as walking beings and come to value walking as a natural, human way of getting from one place to another, a way that is totally economical, pollution-free, and healthy. The modes of transportation that human inventiveness has placed at our disposal will continue to be essential to our society, but we need not despise or neglect walking because of them. Walking deserves to be esteemed more and enjoyed more.

Just Passing Through

By reflecting on the act of walking, I can learn some fundamental truths about human existence in general and my basic relationship to the world I live in. Walking puts me in contact with the ground beneath my feet. At that moment I know that I am and that the solid ground is, and for a moment there is between us a tangible bond. I need the ground to walk on. By walking, I assert my primordial status as a free, self-directed subject able to move through the world at will. Yet I cannot walk on thin air, but only on the ground. I do my own walking, as a unique individual, yet my every step comes down on something that is not me, but something with which my destiny is interwoven. Walking is interaction with the world, give and take with the world. I step forward and the patient ground receives the foot I extend and offers me the resisting surface I need to stand on. To walk is to give and receive in reciprocal interdependence with my environment. At every step I meet the world and the world rises up to meet me. As it is natural for me to walk, so it is natural for me to be situated in an environment that makes activity and life possible for me. I experience my human existence as dependent and situated existence. As I walk over the hard sidewalk or the uneven ruts of a dirt road, I realize that I belong to this scene, that I am somehow part of it. I am not a mere bystander but a participator in the world where I walk; I am not completely separate and indifferent to the ground on which I tread, but one with it in a certain way. I walk mindfully, not indifferently, over the face of the earth. A description of such walking has been given by Thich Nhat Hanh, a Vietnamese Buddhist thinker, in his book *The Miracle of Mindfulness:*

> I like to walk alone on country paths, rice plants and wild grasses on both sides, putting each foot down on the earth in mindfulness, knowing that I walk on the wondrous earth. In such moments, existence is a miraculous and mysterious reality.*

Thich Nhat Hanh sensed something of the mystery of human existence as he walked over "the wondrous earth." To be a human being is to be in passage over the wondrous earth. A human person is a being-in-passage, a wanderer and roamer, not permanently fixed in one place like a tree. I may dwell all my life in the same city or even in the same house, but I am still free to go out and come back as I please. By my going and coming, my mobility within my environment, I vindicate and demonstrate my humanness. As a human being, I am a transient on the earth. I belong to the earth and am interwoven with its past and future history, but at the same time I transcend the limits of earth because I am merely passing over it. The earth cannot claim me totally as its own as long as I have the power to move my feet and continue my journey.

Thus the ordinary act of walking typifies the human condition. Human life from the moment of birth to the moment of death is like a journey on foot across the wondrous earth. Walking tells us that life is passage, or transition. Absolute immobility is death; life lies in activity, and walking is a paradigm of that activity.

Giving Myself Away

Walking can put me in touch not only with the earth and the mystery of being human but with myself, with my identity as an individual. Children in the same family learn to walk at different ages, with different degrees of confidence, and according

---

* Thich Nhat Hanh, *The Miracle of Mindfulness* (Boston: Beacon, 1976), p. 12.

to their own individual style. A personal walking style is per-
fected as one grows older. When I was a youngster I developed
a rapid walking style from frequent walks downtown with my
father, trying to stretch my small legs to match his adult stride.
Usually, I do not notice my brisk style until a companion calls
my attention to it, as happened recently when a friend said after
we had crossed a street, "This is the first time I've had to run to
keep up with someone who's just walking!"

Because I am the individual I am with the history I have, I
walk the way I walk. The link between my personal identity
and my style of walking may not be deliberate and conscious,
but it is definitely present. Walking is such an automatic and
taken for granted activity that it permits my inner identity to
express itself without surveillance by the more conscious dimensions of the self.

People are not usually aware that they give themselves away
by their manner of walking, but others notice it if they are
perceptive enough. If there is a knock on my door and a man
stomps in almost before I have invited him, I can tell before he
says a word that I am dealing with an angry individual. His
aggression is evident from the way he charges into the room.
Perhaps if I confronted him explicitly with his anger he might
deny it: "Who me? I'm not angry." But that would be because
he was not prepared to acknowledge his own feelings, even
though they were evident to an observer.

I can learn to become aware of the way I walk, and then I
can check my feeling state according to my observation. For
instance, I notice myself walking extremely fast, almost running. And I can ask myself whether getting there a few seconds
sooner should really be that important to me. Why am I so
driven? Or I notice myself strolling leisurely along, glancing to
right and to left at every step. I can check my feelings and say,
"Yes, I am in a happy-go-lucky mood today," and then enter
into the mood more fully if I wish. Perhaps I catch myself more
than once walking along with my nose in the air, scarcely giving a nod of recognition to those I meet. What does this haugh-
tiness tell me about my relationship to others, about my
unspoken evaluation of others? Am I too reserved, too aloof,

too snobbish? Am I communicating to others the message that I do not want to be bothered?

Unfortunately, one's personal style of walking, like all body language, is somewhat ambiguous both to oneself and to others. Different interpretations are possible, and the true interpretation may be lost to everyone. A rapid pace may indicate a determined will, or mental preoccupation, or fear, or a suddenly remembered obligation, or an urgent call of nature. Still, it can be informative to pay attention to walking styles. If I know my own habitual style, or someone else's habitual style, any variation is easier to note and interpret. The habitual style corresponds to an underlying individuality and temperament, such as laziness, drivenness, cautiousness, recklessness. The occasional variation corresponds to the dominant state at a given moment: this habitually lazy fellow is in a hurry right now.

Differences in walking styles can be noticed also in people from different parts of the country. Watch the way people from the North walk, and then watch Southerners. Exceptions multiply as we generalize further, but observers can sometimes pick out walking styles characteristic of different nationalities and countries. And men and women generally show a difference in walking style due to many factors, including differences in style of shoes and clothing. Individual, national, and cultural differences can all be reflected to some degree in the way people carry themselves as they walk.

Going Walking

When I see a man walking on a lovely afternoon down the sidewalk outside my window, I may speculate to myself, "He's taking advantage of the fine afternoon to be out walking." But I have no way of knowing for sure unless I run after him and ask what brings him out this afternoon. Perhaps he is walking in order to think out some perplexing problem, or to explore a shorter route to his office. People take walks for a variety of reasons, and the classification to be presented in this section is not exhaustive, but the following categories illustrate some potential benefits of going for a walk.

Walking for exercise.   When I was a student in Pittsburgh, I frequently walked to school, a distance of about a mile
and a half. The trek took about half an hour and led down a hill
past picturesque row-houses, across the 10th Street Bridge over
a broad river with frequent barge traffic, then up a long flight of
stairs to the top of the bluff where the university was located.
Sometimes I went alone, but I usually walked with a fellow
student; and often we would meet more students at the bridge,
coming from other directions. This morning exercise, in sun,
rain, and snow, helped keep me alert during the lectures and gave
me a good appetite for lunch. Later, I moved to a section of the
city much further away and had to come to school by bus. I
missed my daily walks; I could feel the lack of exercise in my
body.

Walking is a form of exercise almost universally recommended by medical advisors. A brisk walk brings most of the
body into action, deepens the breathing, and improves blood
circulation throughout the system. The rhythmic motion of the
walk calms tense muscles and nerves. The walker does not need
the elaborate exercising facilities of a health spa, but reaps most
of the same revitalizing benefits for free. Wilderness hiking and
backpacking provide extended periods of exercise for those
who have the time.

Walking for exercise has beneficial effects on the whole person, not just the body. The effects of daily walking for even
twenty minutes can eventually be felt in a more relaxed, flowing style of life as our spirit harmonizes itself with the basic
rhythms of our body, the rhythms of heartbeat, breathing, and
repetitive movement. Monastic life has implicitly recognized
the value of walking for deepened personal integration and for
daily exercise. Traditional monastic architecture provided a rec-
tangular cloister for walking, often enclosing an attractive park
area with trees and fountains. The individual monastic cells of a
Carthusian charterhouse include a hallway called the "ambula-
tory," used specifically for walks.

Walking with a companion.   On my walks to school, I
was usually accompanied by a fellow classmate, whose presence

and conversation contributed greatly to the enjoyment of the walk. Our dialogue ranged leisurely over a variety of topics as we made our way down the hill and over the bridge; at other times we walked together in reflective silence. Walking with a companion can be an enriching and memorable experience, because the walk seems to stimulate ideas and encourage sharing on a deep level. For that reason, a walking companion should be chosen with care and discretion; a good companion would be one who can "match your stride" both in walking and in range of interest. Otherwise, there is disharmony and the walk may soon become tedious or frustrating instead of beneficial.

A variation of walking with a companion would be group walks, such as parades and processions. In a parade or a religious procession, which is a sacred parade, all walk at the pace set by the leader. To the onlooker, all the marchers seem to be moving as one; the perfect unison of their performance draws admiration. To the participant, the pleasure lies in feeling part of a living, moving whole that seems to be sustained by a life and meaning of its own and by a rhythm that might be emphasized in music and song.

Walking to get away. There are times when I prefer not to walk with anyone at all. Instead, I wish to get away from everyone and to forget everything for a time, to be healed and renewed. I wish to leave a situation or place or task that is becoming too much for me, overwhelming me. When I need to get away for awhile, a long solitary walk is often a good solution. Walking, I can regain my sense of identity and personhood simply by being away from the influence of others and their demands and special interests. As I walk, I rediscover my freedom. I had been in danger of being submerged by forces outside my control, and I must still face those forces when I return; but while walking I can rediscover a part of me that remains eternally free. My freedom to walk away is symbolic of something in me that can never be compelled. Walking is pure liberation.

As I distance myself from a stressful situation, I seem to leave it behind me. Walking helps clear the conflict out of my mind and heart and tends to leave me feeling clean and renewed. I can go back and confront the situation with a fresh perspective. Walking has opened other vistas. I see that the world is bigger than my personal problems and projects. Putting down one foot after the other on the solid earth has put me in touch with reality once again. I see my relationship to the whole. The situation may not have changed very much when I return, but I have changed because of my walk. After my walk I feel ready to make a new beginning, as if I had been away on vacation.

Thinking walks.   In this type of walking, I want to take my problems with me instead of leaving them behind. Problems that seem insoluble as I sit at my desk and wrestle with them can sometimes be solved on a walk. Walking helps free the mind from mental blocks and release the flow of ideas. Intuition seems to come alive and answers are seen in a flash of insight. With the rhythmic motion of the walk and the deep, regular breathing, imagination begins to roam playfully over possibilities and impossibilities until finally I hit upon the best solution. Or perhaps something I happen to see distracts my attention for a time, and when I come back to my problem I find that the unconscious, creative processes of my mind have been working all along, and from then on progress is rapid. Mind and body are so linked that they can move together and help each other. The most famous school of philosophers in ancient Greece was called "Peripatetic," because these great thinkers loved to stroll as they pondered the mysteries of the universe; their philosophy evolved as they walked. Of course, walking is not guaranteed to accomplish miracles and supply solutions out of thin air. A thinking walk is often most successful after I have done my deskwork as thoroughly as I can.

Walking to explore.   One of the best ways to get to know a territory is to walk in it. If I fly over it at thirty thousand feet, I may not even see it. If I drive through it at fifty-five miles an hour I will see more, but still miss most of what is there. It is when I explore a territory on foot that I come to know it as it is. The human senses need time to absorb and process new data; by slowing down to a walk, I give myself time to hear and smell and contemplate and get the feel of the land I walk through. As

I walk through new territory I begin to savor the intangible spirit of the place. Then I can say I have truly been there—not when I can produce snapshots of the scenery or the skyscrapers, but when I have walked there and experienced the spirit of the place.

It takes time to explore a place as it deserves. It took Thoreau more than a year to explore Walden Pond, and it took Annie Dillard more than a year to explore Tinker Creek; but those who have read their books are likely to agree that it was time well spent. We learn from such explorers that there is no need to travel to exotic lands in search of exhilarating places to walk. We can begin in our own back yard and discover the most astounding things about our own neighborhood if we learn to walk with docile openness and a sense of wonder.

When I walk to explore, ready to be surprised by the unexpected, I can sense the presence of mystery. When I have made one discovery I never know what I might encounter around the next bend. Contemporary urban society seems to have lost that urge to explore and that feeling for the mystery of things that seem to come so naturally to children and to so-called primitive people. An example from the poetry of the Navajo Indians recorded by Murray Bodo in his book *Walk in Beauty* shows what we may have lost:

> At dawn I walk.
> Behind me it is blessed where I walk,
> Before me it is blessed where I walk,
> I walk, I walk,
> At dawn I walk.

The Navajo walker is enveloped in blessing. As he explored the beginning of a new day he felt completely in harmony with the land where he walked and with the mystery that revealed something of itself in the dawn light.

Walking for joy.   There are times when I do not want to exercise or explore or think or escape; I simply want to go for a walk, to walk for the sheer joy of walking. I have no ulterior purpose or goal beyond walking for a given length of time. I am not going anywhere in particular; all that matters is that I be on the march. This type of walking is spontaneous activity for the sake of the activity itself, and for the aesthetic enjoyment derived from it. Enjoyment comes from the simple things of life as well as from elaborately concocted happenings.

There are unintended benefits to be reaped from a joy walk. I will discover a form of pure recreation, the renewing effect of an organism functioning perfectly in accord with its potentiality. I return recreated, a rejuvenated being. I have touched once again the sources of life: the solid earth, the fresh air that flows around me, the rays of sunshine. I realize that I have not so much taken a walk as given myself to the walk and let the walk take me and transform me. My walk has taken me out of myself and then given me back to myself transformed and full of gladness.

Here we can mention another variation of walking, in the form of dance. Dance, especially ballet, is the poetry of walking. Dance celebrates and glorifies walking by highlighting its dimension of graceful, harmonious movement. The functional aspect of walking is almost entirely absent from dance; the ballerina mincing across the stage on tiptoe is not going anyplace. Dance is exuberantly nonutilitarian; it is a means of self-expression and communication. For instance Shiva, the Lord of the dance, is portrayed with gestures and postures that communicate the doctrines of Hindu mythology. Dancing often expresses the feeling of joy. Adults might say, "I could dance for joy," while children actually do dance with delight, prompted by spontaneous natural impulse. The Old Testament records Miriam dancing for joy at the crossing of the Red Sea, King David dancing before the ark, and the returning exiles dancing for joy when they caught sight of the city of Zion [Exod. 15:20; 2 Sam. 6:14; Jer. 31:13].

Motion on Credit

Our description of walking has stressed how easy and natural this activity is. The more a function lies under our control, the less attention we pay to it. Only when something goes wrong do we give our attention to the matter, until we have it under control once again. If I stumble every time I walk over a new throw-rug on the floor, I will eventually learn to adjust my step a little higher at that point and then I will forget about the rug. If I am walking a rough road in the country and find myself tripping over branches and stones, I will learn that I have to pick up my feet and then there will be no more difficulty. A similar process of adjustment must have taken place when I originally learned to walk as an infant. Infants totter in search of their balance as they master the proper coordination to avoid falling at every step.

If I look closely at the act of walking, I can see that there is indeed a possibility of falling at every step. Every time I step forward there is a moment when I am too far off balance to step back; momentum would make me fall flat on my face if my other leg did not swing forward and find firm support in time to catch the weight of my body. Balance is lost momentarily, then regained. The smooth flow of successive steps conceals the precarious nature of the operation, but a closer look reveals it. "Human gait is, in fact, a continuously arrested falling," says Erwin Straus in his book on *Phenomenological Psychology*.

Once I have accepted this picture of walking, an important implication begins to be clear. Walking involves an implicit act of trust. I take the risk of moving forward because I confidently expect that my leg will find sure footing and quickly restore my balance. If my implicit trust is betrayed by an unseen obstacle or a hole in my path, then I trip and fall. Because the probability of such a fall seems quite remote, I grow accustomed to moving forward with speed and confidence. Eventually I forget that I am moving in confidence and that every step is an act of trust. Thus walking becomes an activity I take for granted and presume is under my absolute control.

The fact of the matter is that I am not totally in control. I walk, ultimately, in faith and trust. Walking, in the words of Erwin Straus, is "motion on credit." To extend the metaphor I might say that my creditor is the ground on which I walk. Most of the time my credit is good and the ground comes to my aid with needed support. But each step involves making a new pact with the ground beneath my feet. I cannot walk totally on my own any more than I can walk on air. Without solid ground beneath my feet, I fall. It takes solid ground plus moving feet to constitute walking. We walk as dependent beings.

Journey in Trust

Human life is a journey. If walking typifies the journey through life, then life is a journey in trust. Life is movement into the unknown future. To a certain extent the future may be predictable, but I cannot see very far ahead, nor around the corners. I do not know for sure what the future will be like till I make my act of faith and step forward, changing future into present reality.

Like walking, life generally is motion on credit. I go forward trusting that things will somehow sort themselves out in the end, despite the present confusion. I go forward believing that there must be a way out of the labyrinth and that somehow I will find it. I do not see my path in the clarity of the noonday sun, but discern it faintly in the twilight. To imagine that life should be full of certainty and security, or that some people must feel perfectly certain and secure even if I do not, is to misunderstand the nature of the human journey. Life is inevitably full of ambiguities and doubts, just as walking is perpetually threatened by pitfalls and stumbling blocks. Yet I can go on walking and go on living in trust and in serene joy.

If for long periods of time my life moves along fairly smoothly, it may happen that the degree of actual trust in my life grows smaller and smaller. Just as it is possible to take for granted my power to walk as I please, so it is possible to take life for granted and to think that I have my life well in control. I become tranquilized in a comfortable, familiar routine that promises to carry me along for the rest of my life like a boat gliding along with the current of a river. I have minimized all foreseeable risks and maximized all possible security. Nothing can trip me now; or almost nothing.

But people with this view of life have already tripped and fallen without knowing it. They were tripping and going down as soon as they thought they had everything under control. Their closed, self-centered style of life will take them nowhere.

To live is to go on a journey and to suffer the vicissitudes and inconveniences of pedestrian travel. For the most part I keep my balance as I go; but it is a moving balance, not the stable balance of one who stands still. The future into which I move is full of the unexpected, but I surrender myself to what the future may bring; what I cannot control I have learned to trust. Basically I place my trust in life: not in myself but in the forward-moving rhythm of life around me, the silent rhythm to which I set my pace.

Walking tells us something about the mystery of human existence, like a mirror held up to reflect the structure of life. In the following sections, we will see whether this same mirror can catch the reflection of our spiritual life as well. Can the mystery of walking help interpret our relationship with the ultimate ground of our being, the God who created us and invites us to walk with him in intimate companionship? In the Old and New Testaments, we can trace the typical course of humanity's wayward relationship with God. There we read the story of God's patient efforts to lead a balking, headstrong people down the right path.

Walking and the Old Testament

Much of the Old Testament is the story of nomadic people. Even after the Israelites became a sedentary people in the towns of Palestine, the frequent pilgrimages to the temple and the annual Feast of Tents kept alive the nomadic tradition. The patriarchs were nomads, moving their livestock from one place to another in search of water and pasturage, never settling permanently anywhere. When famine completely devastated the land, Jacob moved his entire family and all his possessions to Egypt. Generations later, the Lord brought his people back from Egypt under the leadership of the shepherd, Moses. For forty years they wandered through the desert as the Lord molded them into a people he could call his own.

The desert journey was a time of intimacy with the Lord and daily dependence on him. The text anthropomorphically describes Yahweh walking about in the midst of the camp: "Since the Lord, your God, walks to and fro within your camp to defend you and to put your enemies at your mercy, your camp must be holy" [Deut. 23:15]. The Lord made his dwelling place in their midst, in the ark and the tent of meeting, in the cloud by day and the pillar of fire by night: "I will set my dwelling among you, and will not disdain you. Ever walking to and fro in your midst, I will be your God, and you will be my people" [Lev. 26:11–12]. The familiarity of the Lord with his people in the desert renewed the paradisal condition when "the Lord God walked to and fro in the garden at the breezy time of the day" [Gen. 3:8].

The wisdom literature of the Bible took up the theme of God walking, and contrasted his mobility with the immobility of the pagan idols "who have feet but cannot walk" [Ps. 113: 15]. Our God can walk "on the wings of the wind" [Ps. 103:3], on the crests of the sea [Job 9:8], and in the depths of the abyss [Job 38:16]. Anyone who wishes to follow the Lord and come to the place where he dwells must "walk without fault and act with justice" [Ps. 14:2]. The psalmist went on to describe this righteous walk, stressing the virtues of honesty, piety, and fraternal charity, and concluding with the promise that "such a man will stand firm forever" [Ps. 14:5].

Walking and the New Testament

During the years of his public ministry, Jesus was an itinerant preacher walking the roads of Judea and Galilee. When the people of one village tried to persuade him not to leave them, he replied that his mission was "to announce the good news of the reign of God to other towns" [Luke 4:43]. Jesus invited a small group of disciples to be his constant traveling companions. As they walked Jesus answered their questions, explained his parables, and instructed them about his future destiny. St. Luke's gospel makes use of the journey of Jesus and his followers to Jerusalem as a structural device to bring unity and movement to the gospel narrative. The climax of the journey is the triumphal entry into Jerusalem, in a procession led by Jesus mounted on an ass that had been borrowed for the occasion.

In the fourth gospel, walking acquires a metaphorical sense when walking in darkness is contrasted with walking by the light of life. No follower of Jesus walks in darkness; his life and conduct manifest his fellowship with Jesus, the light of the world [John 8:12; 12:35]. John notes that there were some who began to follow Jesus, but then lost confidence in him after his discourse on the bread of life: "From this time on, many of his disciples broke away and would not walk with him any longer" [John 6:66]. In his dialogue with Peter after the resurrection, Jesus contrasted the freedom to walk and the coercion of persecution:

As a young man you fastened your belt and walked about as you pleased but when you are older you will stretch out your hands, and another will tie you fast and lead you where you do not wish to go. [John 21:18]

In the Pauline epistles, walking often refers to conduct and style of life. Paul exhorts the Galatians to "walk according to the spirit" and not yield to the flesh with its sinful passions and desires [Gal. 5:16]. To walk in a way that is "worthy of the Christian calling" or "worthy of the Lord" and pleasing to him is to live humbly and patiently, "bearing with one another lovingly" [Eph. 4:1; Col. 1:10; 1 Thess. 2:12; 4:1]. The figure of darkness and light occurs as the Ephesians are asked to "walk as children of light" [Eph. 5:8]. The nearness of God to his people is expressed with the help of a text from Leviticus: "You are the temple of the living God, just as God has said: 'I will dwell with them and walk among them. I will be their God and they shall be my people' " [Cor. 6:16; Lev. 26:12]. Other New Testament material will be considered in the following section as we study the chief threat to walking, the danger of tripping.

Tripping and Stumbling

We have seen how the physical act of walking depends on bringing one leg forward in time to catch the weight of the body as it falls forward. If there is an unseen obstacle in my path, I will stumble, lose my balance, and fall to the ground. In the spiritual life, I stumble every time I yield to temptation and disobey God's will. At that moment I have fallen into sin and no longer walk before the Lord.

Scripture's word for an occasion of sin or a temptation to sin is "scandal." Scandal literally is the stone over which I trip. Anything that is a scandal to me makes me lose my footing, slip, and fall. The prophets Isaiah, Jeremiah, and Ezekiel all spoke of these stumbling blocks or obstacles in the path [Isa. 57:14; Jer. 6:21; Ezek. 3:20]. In the New Testament, Jesus frequently warned of the danger of scandal:

It would be better for anyone who scandalizes one of these little ones to be drowned by a millstone around his neck. What terrible things will come on the world through scandal! It is inevitable that scandal should occur. Nonetheless, woe to that man through whom scandal comes! [Matt. 18:6–7]

When Peter took Jesus aside and suggested that he might find a way to avoid suffering and death, Peter himself became a scandal and a tempter. Jesus rebuked him harshly: "Get out of my sight, you satan! You are trying to make me trip and fall. You are not judging by God's standards but man's" [Matt. 16:23].

In this episode it was Peter who actually tripped over the stumbling block of Jesus' future passion. Jesus knew that he himself and his words and actions and passion were a scandal that would bring many to their downfall. He declared to the delegation sent by John the Baptist: "Blest is the man who finds no stumbling block in me" [Matt. 11:6]. In his parable of the sower, he predicted that the unstable would eventually fall away: "They have no root; they believe for a while, but fall away in time of temptation" [Luke 8:13]. At the last supper, during a moment of close fellowship, Jesus foretold that even his table companions would lose faith in him and trip: "Tonight you will all be scandalized in me" [Matt. 26:31]. But Jesus knew that after tripping and stumbling they would regain their balance; he looked forward to the time when they would again walk together in Galilee [Matt. 26:32]. In John's gospel, Jesus promised to send a Comforter, the Paraclete, and said: "I have told you all this to keep you from being scandalized" [John 16:1].

St. Paul's experience in attempting to convert his fellow

Jews was that the cross of Jesus continued to be the major stumbling stone. He wrote to the Corinthians: "We preach Christ
crucified—a stumbling block to Jews, and an absurdity to Gen-
tiles, but to those who are called . . . Christ the power of God
and the wisdom" [1 Cor. 1:23]. As he pondered the mystery of
Israel's unbelief, Paul could see the meaning of the Old Testament prophecies:

> They stumbled over the stumbling stone, as Scripture says: "Be-
> hold, I am placing in Zion a stone to make men stumble and a rock to
> make them fall; but he who believes in him will not be put to shame."
> [Rom. 9:32–33]

Within the community of believers, Paul had to contend with
groups that were scandalized by Christians who did not adhere
to the Jewish dietary laws or practice circumcision. Paul related
these scruples to the primary scandal of the cross: "If I were
[preaching circumcision], the cross would be a stumbling block
no more" [Gal. 5:11].

How was it possible to get over the stumbling block and not
be tripped by it? For Paul there was only one way: by a living
faith in "him who raised Jesus our Lord from the dead" [Rom.
4:24]. The model of such faith is Abraham, the father of believers, who trusted in God's promise against all odds, "hoping
against hope" [Rom. 4:18]. With Abrahamic faith in God, I
walk without stumbling. I walk in the footsteps of the nomad
Abraham who began his great walk of faith when he was seven-
ty-five years old and heard God summon him to leave Haran
and set out on foot for the land of Canaan [Gen. 12:1–5]. The
following section will investigate some of the implications for
spirituality that flow from walking in faith and trust.

Walking with God

The physical act of walking can be described as "motion on
credit," as we have seen. Every step I take implies an act of
trust that the ground below me is firm and that my foot will
clear any obstacle. Walking in such terrain as the soft sand of a
lakeshore, a dry streambed, or a desert presents definite prob-

lems. I may feel more secure if I have a walking stick along to lean on. The sand can move out from beneath my feet until I feel I am sinking into a hole. The feeling is one of impotence and uneasiness; I long for firm ground under my feet. A walk like this, on desert sand of Navajo Indian country, has been described by Murray Bodo:

> Your legs ache from the slipping of earth beneath you. There is no solid ground to support your weight and you change the shape of the unstable earth by the simple act of walking. In this desert world it is hard to feel secure and independent; and you reach out for the spirits who live beneath, above, and in all things; you reach for the hand of God, and Indian and White Man are one in poverty and dependence on what transcends the earth.*

God led his chosen people through the desert sand of the Sinai peninsula for forty years in order to bring home to them their radical dependence on him. He permitted them to struggle in order to show them that he was their only security, the divine ground of their being. He wanted them to reach out for his strong, securing hand when they felt themselves foundering in the soft sand. He wanted them to rely on him, lean their weight on him, have total confidence in his saving presence in their midst. God walked in the midst of his people that they might walk with him and he might be their God.

Trust is not an easy lesson to learn. The generation in the desert learned it, but subsequent generations tended to forget. The prophets had to continually prod the people: "Who among you fears the Lord, heeds his servant's voice, and walks in darkness without any light, trusting in the name of the Lord and relying on his God?" [Isa. 50:10]. The more the Lord blest his people with prosperity, the more they attributed it to their own skill and strength. Deutero-Isaiah urged them to find their strength in the Lord: "Though young men faint and grow weary, and youths stagger and fall, they that hope in the Lord will renew their strength . . . they will run and not grow weary, walk and not grow faint [Isa. 40:30–31].

---

* Murray Bodo, *Walk in Beauty* (Cincinnati: St. Anthony Messenger Press, 1974), p. 23.

The wisdom literature of the Bible developed this prophetic theme of relying on the Lord. The ideal relationship between Israel and Yahweh was portrayed in the bridal imagery of the Song of Songs. In one of the scenes the bride and her beloved are described walking together arm in arm as they come from a desert area. The poet exclaimed: "Who is this coming up from the desert, leaning upon her lover?" [Cant. 8:5]. The Hebrew word for leaning has the connotation of "finding strength and stability in." The bride walked with her beloved, supported on the desert sand by his strength, relying on him.

To walk with God, in the biblical sense, implies entrusting oneself unconditionally to the Lord and following his lead. The risk involved in total self-surrender is real enough, because it often means walking with an unseen partner into an unseen future. When I walk with God I am no longer the complete master of my own steps, no longer in control of my own life and the situation around me. The instinct in me that longs for firm ground under my feet has to yield in the risk of faith.

But the venture of faith and trust is rewarded by an incredible familiarity with the Lord. To take another example from the Old Testament, we read in Genesis about a man so close to God that he was taken alive into the kingdom of heaven. This was the antediluvian patriarch Enoch: "The whole lifetime of Enoch was three hundred and sixty-five years. Then Enoch walked with God, and he was no longer here for God took him" [Gen. 5:23–24]. Enoch's life spanned a year of years, a symbol of his perfection. Generations later, he was still remembered as a just man and an example to the pagans because he walked with God: "Enoch was found just, for he walked with God, an example of knowledge to the nations" [Sir. 44:16]. And in the New Testament, the letter to the Hebrews praised Enoch for the faith that made him pleasing to God: "By faith Enoch was taken away without dying. . . . Scripture testifies that, before he was taken up, he was pleasing to God—but without faith it is impossible to please him" [Heb. 11:5–6].

Enoch, who walked with God in the familiarity and the obscurity of faith, almost recovered the paradisal state of Adam and Eve who were accustomed to walking freely with the Lord

God before the first sin. The possibility of intimate union with God lies hidden within the commonplace activity of walking. Walking with God in spirit of living trust can symbolize the highest fulfillment of human destiny. Understood in this fullest sense, walking with God can take place not only when I am strolling outdoors on a contemplative walk, but even when I am flat on my back in a hospital bed; because the essential element is my ongoing union of will with the directive will of God. I walk with God by the steps I take in faith, hope, and love.

Conclusion

Reflection on the ordinary human activity of walking has yielded insights into the deeper meaning of life. On the purely human level, I see that my body was designed to enable me to walk the earth with a confident stride. Walking comes naturally; I am an "itinerant being," in the words of philosopher Gabriel Marcel. From birth to death I am moving about, always going somewhere, a wayfarer, never permanently at rest. Spiritually, on the level of my relationship with God, I am involved in an interior odyssey all my life. I struggle to walk before God and be perfect, as the Lord commanded Abraham and all his descendants [Gen. 17:1]. The many times I stumble teach me to rely more totally on divine assistance. I learn to follow the directives of someone else's will and walk with God, believing in his unseen presence in all the events that happen on my journey. I learn to trust firmly in his guidance through all the trials and doubts and difficulties on the way.

I see the pattern of my life in the Old Testament account of the chosen people slowly making their way across the desert to the holy land that the Lord had promised to give them, a land flowing with milk and honey. I see the pattern again in the New Testament as Jesus walked the dusty roads of Galilee, Samaria, and Judea on his way to meet the destiny that awaited him in Jerusalem. Death and resurrection in Jerusalem was "his appointed course" [Luke 22:22], his way to the Father. No one comes to the Father except by that way; Jesus has led the way, and he said that he himself was "the way" [John 14:6].

To be follower of Jesus is to be a wayfarer, walking the path that leads ultimately to the holy land, to Jerusalem. "So we saunter toward the Holy Land," writes a great American walker, Henry David Thoreau. Perhaps Thoreau was aware of the implications of his phrase, because he carefully explained the meaning of the word "saunter" according to theories then prevalent:

[Saunter] is beautifully derived "from idle people who roved about the country, in the Middle Ages, and asked charity, under pretense of going *a la Sainte Terre,*" to the Holy Land, till the children exclaimed, "There goes a Sainte-Terrer," a Saunterer, a Holy-lander.*

If we say that the Christian vocation is to be a Holy-Lander, we need to understand that we are called not to be in the Holy Land already, but to be on our way there in obedience and trust. It is for God to determine how long our journey will last and under what circumstances we shall finally reach our destination and enter his sabbath rest [Heb. 4:11]. No two Christians walk exactly the same path to Jerusalem, because no two people are exactly the same, though we all follow the footsteps of Christ. Each is faithful to his or her Christian vocation by being faithful to his or her own personal path.

In a sense, we have already arrived at the end of our journey by our will to persevere every step of the way through all difficulties and dangers. Jerusalem is here and now, even as I walk toward it. As I walk I am in the presence of the Lord, doing the will of the Lord, and so I am already standing on the threshold of the house of the Lord. The going is the goal by another name. As I go, and as I am constantly arriving, I join in the "song of ascents" sung by the Israelite pilgrims as they made their way up to Jerusalem for the festival:

---

* Henry David Thoreau, "Walking," in *Atlantic Monthly* (June 1862), reprinted in Aaron Sussman and Ruth Goode, *The Magic of Walking* (New York: Simon & Schuster, 1967), p. 242; see also p. 249. This book, in addition to the authors' own discussion of walking, contains a 160-page survey of literature on the subject. My own thinking found a major stimulus in this work.

I rejoiced when they said to me,
"We are walking to the house of the Lord."
And now our feet are standing
inside your gates, O Jerusalem! [Ps. 122:2]

The marching song makes the ascent seem easier and lifts the
spirits of the walkers. We walk into an unseen future, rejoicing:

Then were our faces full of laughter,
    and our tongues with shouts of joy!
Then they said among the heathen:
"Great things has Yahweh done for them."
    And we were rejoicing! [Ps. 126:2–3]

SOURCES

Berenice, Sr. "Glorify God in Your Body." *Desert Call* 12, no. 2
    (1977).

Bodo, Murray. *Walk in Beauty*. Cincinnati: St. Anthony Messenger
    Press, 1974.

Bromily, Geoffrey, ed. *Theological Dictionary of the New Testament*,
    s.v. "odos", "pateo"; "pipto", "poreiomai"; "skandalon." Grand
    Rapids: Eerdmans, 1964–1976.

Straus, Erwin. *Phenomenological Psychology*. New York: Basic Books,
    1966.

Sussman, Aaron, and Ruth Goode. *The Magic of Walking*. New York:
    Simon & Schuster, 1967.

4 Resting

. . . .

After the exertion of a vigorous walk, it feels good to sit down and rest. The simple act of flopping down in a comfortable chair and relaxing for a few minutes is another example of a common, ordinary experience that can open up unexpected horizons when we consider it more closely. Rest has much to teach us about human life and about our life with God.

Almost every living thing follows a law of alternating activity and repose. The repose phase is not absolute total inactivity, which would be death, but a slowed down, diminished activity that varies in degree and duration. Plant life enters a period of dormancy during the winter and awakens with a burst of new growth in the spring. Animals, even insects, need periodic resting intervals. Human beings are unable to sustain continuous activity and require a certain amount of rest, including sleep, but the amount is variable. The inability to rest normally is a type of disease called hyperkinesis, often found among children of elementary school age who give a dizzying impression of being in perpetual motion.

Rest is a completely normal, necessary, healthful, and enjoyable occupation, but sometimes we feel in ourselves and see in others—not only in hyperactive children but in mature adults—a resistance to resting. There are incessant pressures from the culture we live in urging us to *do* something, and preferably to buy something or produce something. We may respond by pushing ourselves to the limit, until we are overwhelmed with fatigue. The requirements of economic survival prevent many from resting adequately even if they wanted to. A proverb in the Bible speaks of rest as a luxury the poor cannot afford: "A little sleep, a little slumber, a little folding of the hands to rest, and poverty will come upon you like a robber" [Prov. 24:33]. Time, we have learned, means money, and we are in danger of considering rest a waste of time and an economic loss.

Our basic human need for periodic rest and relaxation is usually enough to overcome the resistance and reluctance we may feel towards taking time off from work. An annual vacation is customary, in addition to holidays during the year. But are vacations restful? Or do we work at taking a vacation with the same drivenness and intensity with which we throw ourselves into other tasks, so that we arrive back from vacation more exhausted than we were when we left? Do we really know how to rest when we want to? Or is it impossible, after all, to make of resting a project to accomplish at will?

This line of questioning suggests that we should deepen our understanding of the phenomenon of rest. What do we mean when we speak of "rest"? What can we learn about rest from other cultures or from a repository of wisdom such as the Bible? The following sections will discuss several aspects of resting, with the intention of gradually leading the discussion to the deepest level of meaning where the human person finds ultimate rest in the divine.

Understanding Rest

Going back to the initial example, what is happening when I sit down in a favorite chair to rest after a vigorous walk? I have stopped doing what I was doing and for the moment am quite content to do nothing but relax. Rest seems to imply the cessation of activity coupled with a feeling of contentment or enjoyment. Rest might be described as enjoyable inactivity. This description of rest may have to be nuanced as we consider the matter more deeply; but, for the present, "enjoyable inactivity" furnishes an adequate concept, and the picture of a figure stretched out in an easy chair furnishes a mental image of resting.

Sleep can be a form of complete resting, but I can also rest in my chair without falling asleep. Sleep does not always bring rest; after a night of fitful, worried sleep, I may awaken more exhausted than when I went to bed. And there are people who suffer from a sleeping sickness, a permanent lethargy that makes them want to sleep but never permits them to feel rested and restored by sleeping. Normally, however, sleep is a refreshing and enjoyable form of rest.

Rest may also be distinguished from recreation, although rest does have a restorative, recreative effect. Recreation can take highly active forms in sports and other types of play that can be physically exhausting. After a tennis match or an exhausting "vacation," I feel a need for rest in order to replenish my energy.

There are other levels of the self beyond the physical; rest, as enjoyable inactivity, affects the ego-personal and spiritual levels as well. The culture we live in (especially in urban centers, but elsewhere too) is a fast-moving, stress-filled existence. We learn to function in this culture at the same rate as those around us, juggling three or more different projects simultaneously; but this way of living puts a strain on us psychologically, emotionally, and mentally. Physically we may not be overly active, but we experience a great need for rest because of the strain of living in the modern world. Rest will help us feel like ourselves again, but a lasting result will come only when we have reexamined our lifestyle and learned to live more harmoniously in the situation we choose for ourselves.

On the spiritual level of the self, we are subject to restlessness and dissatisfaction if we are out of harmony with our own deepest center. Physical rest can be helpful only indirectly here, and may even be a hindrance by providing a temporary escape. When I am asleep I am not bothered by guilt feelings, depression, failings, difficult decisions, troublesome interpersonal relationships. The kind of resting that brings peace to the spirit is the quieting of our numerous desires in a supremely fulfilling love. In the famous words of St. Augustine to his Lord, "You have made us for yourself and our hearts are restless till they rest in you." More will be said about resting in God when we reflect on biblical material.

It will be helpful to relate the phenomenon of rest to a concept that we find in oriental culture, in the Chinese ethical system of Taoism. In the fourth century B.C., philosopher Lao Tzu compiled a handbook for wise rulers called the *Tao Te Ching*. Lao Tzu was convinced that the wisdom of governing lay in adopting a course of action so completely in harmony with the aspirations of the people and the requirements of the situation that the ruler seemed not to be acting at all, like a jade worker whose instrument leaves no mark on the precious stone but simply unfolds its inner beauty. The name given to this actionless activity is *wu-wei*, literally "without action." *Wu-wei* goes beyond our understanding of rest as enjoyable inactivity and integrates restfulness into activity itself by pointing to a way of action that is always in perfect harmony with the agent, the circumstances, and the nature of the task. As Lao Tzu put it: "In the pursuit of the way [*Tao*] one does less every day; one does less and less until one does nothing at all, and when one does nothing at all there is nothing that is undone." In paradoxical language, Lao Tzu was speaking about a leisurely, restful approach to activity that is far from mere idleness and inertia. When Lao Tzu called for "action which consists in taking no action," he was suggesting that we might go about our daily life in a way that is deeply restful because completely natural and harmonious, without striving and straining after impossible ideals, without craving for unattainable satisfaction, without anxiety or fear for the future. *Wu-wei* is inspired by a profound trust in the rightness of the way things fundamentally are in human nature and in the world around us.

Some generations after Lao Tzu, the Chinese philosopher Chuang Tzu added to *wu-wei* the note of enjoyment that we have already observed in rest as enjoyable inactivity. Chuang Tzu wrote as follows, according to Thomas Merton's translation of *The Way of Chuang Tzu:*

> From [the sages'] stillness comes their non-action [*wu-wei*] which is also action. And is therefore, their attainment. For stillness is joy.

Joy is free from care, fruitful in long years. Joy does all things without concern; for emptiness, stillness, tranquillity, tastelessness, silence and non-action are the root of all things.*

Chuang Tzu is saying that *wu-wei* includes joy or contentment because it is radically free from care or concern about these feelings or any feelings. Happiness happens when we cease to act with a view to obtaining it. If we are still concerned and still desiring anything, we are not perfectly at rest, perfectly tranquil and serene. "Here is how I sum it up," said Chuang Tzu:

> Heaven does nothing: Its non-doing [*wu-wei*] is its serenity. Earth does nothing: its non-doing is its rest. From the union of these two non-doings all actions proceed, all things are made. How vast, how invisible this coming-to-be! All things come from nowhere! How vast, how invisible—no way to explain it! All beings in their pefection are born of non-doing. Hence it is said "Heaven and earth do nothing yet there is nothing they do not do." Where is the man who can attain to this non-doing?**

We have already seen in what sense *wu-wei* can bring about the harmonious unfolding of potentialities in a leisurely, actionless way; but what is remarkable in this ancient Chinese text is that the attainment of *wu-wei* by human beings is considered possible only as a participation in the divine rest, the *wu-wei* of heaven and earth, the fruitful restfulness of *Tao,* supreme master.

As I reflect on these texts, I begin to see new horizons open up within the phenomenon of rest. Far more seems to be involved in rest than the simple action of slipping off one's shoes and flopping down in a comfortable chair after coming back from a vigorous walk. This ordinary, everyday activity—or inactivity—of resting is intrinsically mysterious. I am not so sure that I know how to rest, especially in the sense of *wu-wei,* joyful, restful activity. To try to be joyfully, restfully active seems futile from the start because I know I cannot force myself to rest without making rest into another form of work. Instead

---

* Thomas Merton, trans., *The Way of Chuang-Tzu* (New York: New Directions, 1965), pp. 101–102.
    ** Ibid.

of asking rest to tell us about itself, let us see in the following section what rest can tell us about ourselves and about human existence in general.

Beings That Rest

We are beings that move and work but we are also beings that rest. For the sake of wholeness I have to befriend both these aspects of my being and not stress activity to the point of crowding out rest, nor value rest to the point of indolence. I am grateful for being able to *do,* as well as to rest. Imagine a person who has survived his or her third heavy stroke and is paralyzed from the neck down. He or she must be fed through a stomach tube because of being unable to swallow either liquid or solid food. The power of speech is gone, and the person can only moan or blink the eyelids in communication. Doctors say that this condition may last for quite some time, a condition of enforced rest with almost total immobility. I am grateful to be able to freely choose either to rest or to move about and talk or feed myself, and I realize that when my power of action or my power of resting is taken away the effect is dehumanizing. Unending work and unending rest are both deadening.

A fully human life seems to be one in which there is an alternation between a more or less active and a more or less passive mode of being. I pump a bicycle up the hill and coast down the other side. I work hard for a promotion or a raise or a new car or new house, and when I obtain the object of my longing I celebrate and feel greatly satisfied. But soon another desire forms in my heart and I become restless again until I attain it. The periods of restful enjoyment come as the fulfillment or reward of my efforts and they last until I am recharged and ready for action once more.

People have varying degrees of need for rest and varying styles or ways of resting, according to their physical and psychological make-up as individuals. There is no universal pattern that can be recommended as best for everyone when it comes to resting, any more than when it comes to working. Resting and working both claim a rightful place in human life. Resting belongs to the reality of being human, just as activity does.

During periods of action I am involved with others and with the world around me in a give-and-take fashion, acting and being acted upon in return. By contrast, when I am at rest, my relationship with the world is one of giving in and giving up, surrendering, yielding, and letting go. In order to rest, I have to renounce temporarily all agent and manipulative purposes. I am still related to the rest of the world through the chair on which I am resting and the voices of others that I may hear, but my involvement is minimal. For the present, I have stopped interacting and am resting contentedly. Rest renounces participation in favor of a more passive role. Rest flows in harmony with the stream of life, no longer directive or controlling. In that moment of profound harmony, restoration takes place, energies are replenished, wounds are healed, anxiety is soothed, and life takes on new meaning.

In our reflections on walking we observed that an act of trust is implicit in every step that we take. To rest is also to trust. To stop and rest is to trust that the world will go on in an orderly fashion without my help for a few minutes or a few hours. I let go of the reins of my life in confidence that things will still be in place when I am ready to take up the reins again. As long as I am resting, life is out of my control. When I rest I commit myself to a friendly world, exposed, defenseless, off guard. A child resting on its mother's breast is the image of perfect security, perfect trust.

If a person is afraid of imminent danger, rest is impossible. Fears are a prime cause of insomnia. The nightmares of children trying to sleep in the dark are sometimes the result of insecurity and fear. If I feel insecure, surrounded by a hostile and threatening world, I cannot afford to let my guard down or be caught napping. Resting means taking a risk, the risk of losing everything in a moment of carelessness. People who feel compelled to cling to the instruments of management and control are not people who experience the comfort of peaceful rest.

Rest seems to come most easily to those who are prepared to let go. We "drop off" to sleep by letting go, as if rolling down a hillside into a grassy meadow. Choosing to rest is a free surrender of self to the mysterious process of restoration that happens to all who give themselves to it. The path to restful harmony with the mystery of life is open to those willing to confide themselves to the unknown, and is closed to those who are not yet prepared to yield or commit themselves.

Because rest carries connotations of trustful surrender and tranquility, the word came to be used as a synonym for contemplative prayer in one tradition of spirituality. The Greek word for rest, *hesychia,* describes the orientation of the hesychast school of prayer represented by John Climacus, Philotheus of Sinai, the monks of Mount Athos, and Russian mystics like Theophan the Recluse. Contemplative prayer often implies a quiet, receptive openness to the presence of the divine. The hesychast ideal was a state of prayer characterized by harmony, unity, silence, tranquility of the mind, the heart and the passions in a totally integrating love of God. In a word, their ideal was rest in God, *hesychia.* The ideal presupposed the preliminary work of self-discipline and ethical responsibility, as well as the practice of continual prayer. Gradually, the hesychasts moved toward perfect harmony with the mysterious center and origin of their being, the experience of God in *hesychia.*

At this point we see the farthest limits of our destiny as beings who rest: we are beings who are able to rest in the sheltering mystery of the divine. The pages of sacred scripture can help us deepen this insight into the phenomenon of rest.

Rest in the Context of the Old Testament

According to the first creation story in Genesis, in six successive days God made heaven and earth and all they contain. Surveying everything he made, God found it very good. Then as if he wished to sit back and enjoy his handiwork, "he rested on the seventh day from all the work he had undertaken" [Gen. 2:2]. The revelation that the living God climaxed his creative activity by resting is a statement so unexpected that we may be tempted to smile; yet the implications of this truth are enormous, even discounting the anthropomorphic language and the fact that Genesis was written fairly late in Israel's history.

If we reflect on the creation narrative as we have it, God's rest seems to spring from a free choice to pause and enjoy his accomplishment rather than from a need to recover his creative energy. His is not the rest of the exhausted worker who comes in, flops down dead tired on his bed without pausing to remove his shoes, and promptly drops off into oblivious sleep. Instead, God's rest is depicted as the celebration of having achieved an intricate, challenging task, as a child might sit back and watch with delight as an electric train begins to move by itself around the elaborate track he has so carefully laid out for it. God paused on the seventh day to rest in satisfaction, fulfillment, contentment, and wonder. The dominant mood seems one of delight in exhilarating creativity and in the incredibly beautiful world brought into being out of nothing. God's rest was his jubilation at the sight of everything being so "very good." "So God blessed the seventh day and made it holy, because on it he rested from all the work he had done in creation" [Gen. 2:3].

Because on the seventh day God rested, his chosen people were commanded to observe the sabbath as a day without work, a day of "complete rest, sacred to the Lord; anyone who does work on the sabbath day shall be put to death" [Exod. 31:15]. In the course of history, other motives were added to enhance the sacredness of the sabbath rest. Thus the sabbath was to be a reminder of liberation from slave work in Egypt, when God led his people out of bondage with his strong hand and outstretched arm [Deut. 5:15]. The sabbath was also a reminder of the promised land that God set apart for his people as their inheritance and their resting place after the wandering in the desert and after exile in Babylon [Deut. 12:9; Jer. 6:16].

Work was forbidden on the day of rest, but the sabbath was intended to be celebrated with joy, with eating and drinking, making love, lighting special candles, holding instruction and worship services, inviting guests. "If you call the sabbath a delight and the Lord's day honorable," said Isaiah, "then you shall delight in the Lord" [Isa. 58:13–14]. The spirit of the commandment to rest was an interior attitude of rejoicing in God's care, trusting dependence on him, renewed dedication to him, and freedom from fear and insecurity by remembrance of his saving deeds. The exterior sabbath observance, which grew stricter and more detailed over the centuries, should have fostered the interior sabbath rest in God.

In fact, however, the sabbath rest was not always well kept exteriorly or interiorly. In the second century A.D., Rabbi Shimon ben Jochai was convinced that, "If Israel would only keep two sabbaths as ordained, redemption would come." The prophets had long before accused Israel of profaning the sabbath by following their own pursuits on the Lord's holy day [Ezek. 22:8; Neh. 13:17; Isa. 56:2]. In the typical pattern, the people would violate the sabbath covenant [Exod. 31:16], God would punish them, they would turn again to the Lord, and he would restore their fortunes. Because they were unwilling to rest, God punished his people by means of restless wandering in exile far from the land of rest that was their inheritance [2 Chron. 36:2–21]. In exile, the people learned that rest is not merely a command but also a gift of the Lord. The totally satisfying rest that is in fact a participation in God's own rest is a gift. Even the rest that consists in dwelling securely in one's own land is God's gift. Jeremiah promised that Israel would return from exile and be given rest:

> As Israel comes forward to be given his rest,
>   the Lord appears to him from afar:
> "With age-old love I have loved you;
>   so I have kept my mercy toward you.
> Again I will restore you,
>   and you shall be rebuilt, O virgin Israel." [Jer. 31:2–4]

According to another promise: "My people will live in peaceful country, in secure dwellings and quiet resting places" [Isa. 32:18]. By God's favor, his people enjoyed such rest, "every man under his own vine or under his own fig tree, undisturbed" [Mic. 4:4].

The rest that God gave to Israel as a nation was experienced in the lives of individuals as a state of enjoying God's favor, a gift of salvation and security. "Thus said the Lord God, the Holy One of Israel: By waiting and by calm you shall be saved, in quiet and in trust your strength lies" [Isa. 30:15]. Jeremiah extended a similar invitation: "Ask the pathways of old which is the way to good, and walk it; thus you will find rest for your souls" [Jer. 6:16]. Even the lowly and the poor could experience God's saving rest: "In my pastures the poor shall eat, and the needy lie down to rest in safety" [Isa. 14:30].

In the Old Testament, rest was a word used on many different but related levels of meaning; from rest as sleep [Eccles. 2:23] or as a euphemism for death or Sheol [Job 3:13], to the sabbath rest, the promised land as rest, and rest as salvation. God was teaching his people that there is more to resting than cessation from work. He was inviting his covenant partner, Israel, to experience the full range of being human, both activity and repose. God himself could act or rest in succession, as Genesis described him resting after the work of creation, or could integrate action and rest as when he dwelt among his people as their protector. The ark of the covenant was thought to be the place of God's localized presence. During the desert wandering and until the time of King Solomon, the ark was sheltered in a tent [2 Sam. 7:6]. During the monarchy, Jerusalem became the central city of worship, and the temple became the permanent resting place of the ark of God's presence. "Go up, Lord, to the place of your rest, you and the ark of your strength. . . . For the Lord has chosen Zion; he has desired it for his dwelling: 'This is my resting-place for ever, here have I chosen to live' " [Ps. 132:8, 13–14]. There, in the temple above the ark, God's name and glory rested. Other texts counterbalanced the theme of rest by insisting that the God who rests is at the same time the God who acts, and that no manmade temple can contain him or prevent him from accompanying his people wherever they may go [1 Kings 8:27; 9:3; Isa. 66:1]. The doctrine of the Old Testament on divine and human rest leads into the New Testament revelation of the Word of God who became flesh and set up his tent among us in the person of Jesus Christ [John 1:14].

Rest in the Context of the New Testament

Jesus came to open for us the way to life in all its fullness. By his own manner of life, as well as his teaching, he has shown us how to live. "Learn from me," he promised, "and you will find rest for your souls" [Matt. 11:29]. We will see what we can learn about rest from the gospels, and then from other parts of the New Testament.

The gospels.   In the gospels, Jesus appears as a man subject to the limitations of his own physical ability and those of the culture and times in which he lived; yet he also enjoys a freedom that enables him to transcend those limitations at will. For most of his life he must have kept the prescribed sabbath rest as everyone else did. Even during his public ministry he attended the synagogue on the sabbath [Mark 1:21]. But he also set aside the customary prohibitions and permitted others to do the same whenever there was danger of forgetting that "the sabbath was made for man, not man for the sabbath" [Mark 2:27].

During the public ministry, Jesus was able to sustain long periods of intense activity, and even to spend whole nights in prayer. Perhaps, as a master of restful activity, Jesus found these experiences of ministering to the needy and of communing with his Father in solitude to be as deeply refreshing as the usual forms of rest [see John 4:34]. Still, Jesus did experience fatigue and feel the need for normal physical rest. "Tired from his journey he sat down at the well" in the Samaritan town of Shechem [John 4:6]. Tired from a long day of preaching and healing, Jesus fell "sound asleep on a cushion" in a fishing boat even during a bad squall [Mark 4:38]. A scribe who wanted to accompany him was warned, "The Son of Man has nowhere to lay his head" [Matt. 8:20]. The verb for "lay, rest, or recline" in this verse comes back when Jesus finally let his head drop in the rest that is death: "Then he bowed his head and delivered over his spirit" [John 19:30]. After death his body was laid to rest in a new tomb [Mark 23:53]. The day of rest in the tomb before the resurrection was a sabbath day, the seventh day, the day after Jesus had completed the work he had undertaken [see Gen. 2:2]. Luke's gospel stresses the motif of rest on this sabbath with reference to the women who witnessed Jesus' burial: "They observed the sabbath as a day of rest, in accordance with the law" [Luke 23:56]. Luke stressed it again in his book of Acts, with a well-chosen quotation from Ps. 16:9: "My body,

too, will rest in hope" [Acts 2:26; verb used also in Luke 13:9].
Rest can bear the connotation of quiet, patient, but expectant
waiting.

Jesus was sensitive to the need that others felt for rest [see
Mark 14:38, 41]. We can reflect on the scene when the apostles
returned in jubilation after the success of their first missionary
journey. In their excitement, as they told Jesus all they had
done, they forgot their own weariness. The crowds were re-
lentless in their demands, "making it impossible for them to so
much as eat" [Mark 6:31]. Jesus decided it was time for a vacation and said to the apostles: "Come by yourselves to an out-of-
the-way place and rest a little" [Mark 6:31]. They got into their
boat and pushed out into the Sea of Galilee. But the crowds
guessed where they were going and made their way to the place
by land. "Upon disembarking Jesus saw a vast crowd. He pit-
ied them, for they were like sheep without a shepherd" [Mark
6:34]. Out of pity, Jesus spoke to them and then fed the entire
crowd with five loaves and two fish. His sensitivity to their
need for refreshment and rest showed when he told his apostles
"to make the people sit down on the green grass in groups or
parties" [Mark 6:39]. The previous reference to sheep, and the
image of the people resting on the green grass, recalls the
prophet's description of the divine Shepherd of Israel:

Thus says the Lord God: I myself will look after and tend my
sheep. . . . They shall lie down on good grazing ground, and in rich
pastures shall they be pastured on the mountains of Israel; I myself will
pasture my sheep; I myself will give them rest, says the Lord God."
[Ezek. 34:11, 14–15]

Ezekiel goes on to say that the Shepherd of Israel shows
particular tenderness towards the lost, the strayed, the injured,
and the sick [Ezek. 34:16]. In just such a context, we find the
gospel's most sublime statement about rest, when Jesus cried
out to the multitude:

Come to me, all you who are weary and find life burdensome, and
I will give you rest. Take my yoke upon your shoulders and learn
from me, for I am gentle and humble of heart. Your souls will find
rest, for my yoke is easy and my burden light. [Matt. 11:28–30]

Jesus extended his invitation to all, but especially to the weary and the heavily burdened, the lowly and the lonely, the poor of Yahweh who are addressed in the beatitudes, the ordinary and unnotable people, and those who place their hope and trust in the God who saves and shepherds his people. In these verses it is still possible to detect the parallelism common in the structure of semitic pronouncements. Repeating the thought of "weary and burdened," the second sentence has the phrase "gentle and humble of heart." In other words, Jesus invited the multitude to come and learn from him, because he knew their condition from the inside; he knew weariness as they knew weariness, but he also knew the secret of rest.

What is this "rest" that Jesus promised to give? In the thought of Jesus, the term rest expanded to its fullest meaning, as the condition that will satisfy the deepest longing of the human heart. We can see in this word *rest* a synonym for the entire work of salvation that Jesus came to accomplish. He could promise rest because he could grant salvation. Rest joins a number of other key words by which Jesus described his salvific mission: water, life, bread, light, truth, peace.

What were the people asked to do that they might enjoy rest? How were they to come to Jesus and learn of him? The path that leads to rest was described paradoxically, in the language of toil: "Take my yoke upon your shoulders . . . for my yoke is easy and my burden light." The yoke was a common metaphor for the observances of the Mosaic law. Jesus may have wished to offer in exchange the yoke of his new law of love [see 1 John 5:3]. He may also have intended a reference to the cross, the crossbeam of which was carried on the shoulders like a yoke to the place of execution. The way to perfect rest lies in acceptance of the cross: "If anyone wishes to come after me, he must deny his very self, take up his cross, and follow in my steps" [Mark 8:34]. To all who are willing to share the burden of his yoke, Jesus offered a sharing in his own rest.

We have seen that Jesus experienced the normal alternation of physical activity and physical rest. If the gospel presents Jesus as a man of action, we also sense in him a deep reservoir of calm, of serenity, of undisturbed rest that helped give his action its unique power and authority. In Jesus rest was an almost tangible aura, like the divine favor or good pleasure that was manifested at his baptism in the Jordan and his transfiguration on the mountain: "This is my beloved Son on whom my favor rests" [Matt 17:5]. Because of what rested on him, Jesus knew what rest means and could impart rest to others by extending God's own love to them: "Anyone who loves me will be true to my word, and my Father will love him: we will come to him and make our resting place with him" [John 14:23]. Whoever abides in God's love, abides also in God's rest [1 John 4:12–16].

Outside the gospels. There are significant statements about rest in the letter to the Hebrews and in Revelation. Both these writings are usually dated after the synoptic gospels, and perhaps at a time when Christians were openly persecuted by the Roman government. In their longing for relief, they began to associate the notion of rest with the kingdom of heaven.

In the third and fourth chapters of the letter to the Hebrews, we find a Christian interpretation of the sabbath rest based on several verses of Psalm 95. This psalm refers to the complaints of the chosen people against God during the crossing of the desert, and their subsequent punishment when the entire generation was forbidden to enter the land of rest, the promised land. "Today, if you should hear his voice," says the psalmist, do not harden your hearts in disobedience and unbelief [Heb. 3:7–8; Ps. 95:8]. The author of Hebrews reasons that the word "today" implies a promise still open to faithful believers. Because of disbelief, God was angry with the generation Moses had led out of Egypt and he swore: "They shall never enter into my rest" [Heb. 3:11; Ps. 95:11]. Eventually, the Hebrews under Joshua did enter the land of Canaan, but the psalmist long afterward declared the promise still open to all who hear God's voice "today." "Therefore a sabbath rest still remains for the people of God," like the sabbath on which God rested from the work of creating [Heb. 4:9, 4]. It is God's own rest that the faithful are invited to enter today. The author drew his conclusion: "Let us strive to enter into that rest, so that no one may fall, in imitation of Israel's unbelief" [Heb. 4:11]. God's rest is presented as a future goal, but one that we are already begin-

ning to enter by heeding the divine word spoken to us today
[see Heb. 4:3, present tense].

What is that divine word that invites all who listen with an
open heart? Could the author of Hebrews have had in mind the
gospel verse we have reflected on: "Come to me, all you who
are weary and find life burdensome, and I will give you rest"
[Matt. 11:28]? Countless voices cajole the human heart with a
promise of rest and fulfillment. Today's advertising industry
thrives on finding new ways of saying, "Come to me, all of
you." Most of us have to learn by experience that these enticements lead to dead ends, disappointments, and further restlessness. There is only one voice whose promise is worthy of full
acceptance and obedience. The author of Hebrews leaves us
with a word of caution: "While the promise of entrance into his
rest still holds, we ought to be fearful of disobeying lest any of
you be judged to have lost his chance of entering" [Heb. 4:1].

The final book of the New Testament, the book of Revelation, refers briefly to the heavenly kingdom of God as a time
and place of rest. There seems to be an allusion to the promise
of Jesus when John writes:

> I heard a voice from heaven say to me: "Write this down: Happy
> now are the dead who die in the Lord!" The Spirit added, "Yes, they
> shall find rest from their labors. . . ." [Rev. 14:13]

By contrast, the punishment for those who worship the beast is
that they shall enjoy no rest either by day or by night [Rev.
14:11]. In the description of the heavenly liturgy, another kind
of activity goes on without rest, the worship of the One seated
on the throne and of the Lamb. Day and night the four living
creatures never rest from their work of praise, continually repeating: "Holy, holy, holy is the Lord God Almighty, He who
was, and who is, and who is to come!" [Rev. 4:8]. The rest
enjoyed by the faithful who die in the Lord is not perpetual
inactivity, but the fullness of life and perfect action, an experience that refreshes and never wearies, the joy of eternal restful
activity in God.

Eternal rest is one of many metaphors that have been
pressed into service to express the ultimate fulfillment of human

longing. Other metaphors abound in early Christian writings, in paintings in the catacombs, on tombstone inscriptions, in the biographies of the martyrs; for example: play, dance, singing, harvest, feasting, marriage. The thought of resting eternally seems unendurable to some people even after rest has been described as a joyfully restful activity. Eternity, however, is not time in duration but time standing still, as we ourselves experience it occasionally when we are intensely present to another human person in a shared experience of joy, beauty, or love. To enter God's rest is an experience of intimacy when time stands still and God rests in us as we rest in God. In the Song of Songs, the bride lost all sense of time as she rested in the shadow of her beloved, his right arm embracing her [Cant. 2:3–7].

Conclusion

I have considered a wide range of meanings in the phenomenon of rest, beginning with physical resting and extending as far as a participation in God's own rest. It is easier now to appreciate the truth of St. Augustine's observation in the first chapter of his *Confessions,* that our hearts are restless until they finally come to rest in God who made us. Possessing God is perfect rest, but there are other forms of resting.

When I rest I cease working and struggling in order to appreciate and enjoy life in itself, life as it is with all its harshness and its beauty, life as it is permitted to unfold according to the design of an infinitely wise and competent creator who found all that he had made to be "very good." When I rest, I do as God did on the seventh day of creation. I stop operating, achieving, managing, controlling, planning, and defending in order simply to be, to savor the fullness of who, what, and where I am in this created universe. To rest is to be content to go on being as I am. God who enjoys the fullness of being is his own rest, as he is also constantly sustaining and caring for all he has made.

When I rest, when I stop doing things, I allow unexpected things to be done in, around, and through me. Rest permits refreshment, healing, integrating, harmonizing to take place. In the passivity of my resting, other powers are able to operate for my benefit. The result is often a surprising discovery that things go better when I let them be. To realize that my action after a certain point has been obstructive and my inaction has been most advantageous is growth in wisdom; but it is also threatening to my self-importance. Resting must teach me that it is not so much what I do that makes me worthwhile as what I am; for I am always more than I do in life, or fail to do. Life itself is always more than it appears at first glance, as we are discovering in our investigation of the mystery of the ordinary.

SOURCES

Bacchiocchi, Samuele. *From Sabbath to Sunday*. Rome: Pontifical Gregorian University Press, 1977.

———. *Rest for Modern Man*. Nashville: Southern Publishing Association, 1976.

Bauer, J. B., ed. *Sacramentum Verbi,* s.v. "Rest"; "Sabbath." New York: Herder & Herder, 1970.

Dumm, Demetrius. "Work and Leisure: Biblical Perspectives." *American Benedictine Review* 28, no. 4 (December 1977).

Friedrich, Gerhard, ed. *Theological Dictionary of the New Testament,* s.v. "Sabbath." Grand Rapids: Eerdmans, 1971.

Guerin, Ellen. *Spirituality and Fatigue*. Unpublished master's thesis, Center for the Study of Spirituality, Institute of Formative Spirituality, Duquesne University, Pittsburgh, 1977.

Lao Tzu. *Tao Te Ching*. Trans. and intro. D. C. Lau. Baltimore: Penguin, 1963.

Léon-Dufour, Xavier, ed. *Dictionary of Biblical Theology,* s.v. "Rest." 2d rev. ed. New York: Seabury Press, 1973.

Merton, Thomas. *The Way of Chuang Tzu*. New York: New Directions, 1965.

Steindle-Rast, David. "The Monk in Us." *Earth's Answer*. Lindisfarne: Harper & Row, 1976.

5 Standing Up

My brisk, energetic walk was followed by a period of rest in a comfortable chair. After sitting there long enough to feel refreshed, I may decide to go into the kitchen for a glass of cold water and perhaps something to nibble on. Action follows decision, and in a moment I am up from the chair and on my feet. For an instant, before turning toward the kitchen, I stand still.

If a photograph had captured that instant of time, it would have shown nothing more extraordinary than a man standing fully erect and poised for movement. My physical ability to assume an upright posture is completely taken for granted. Yet in rising to my feet and standing there, I have carried out an activity that can be seen as expressive of my humanness and also as deeply symbolic of my aspirations and of my graced ability to enter a relationship with God most high. Standing up is an ordinary activity that opens upon mystery if we take the time to investigate it from various points of view.

Idiomatic usage of the word "stand" already indicates different levels of meaning in this term. For example, I may decide to "take a stand" on some matter. Taking a stand implies that I have considered the options, made a judgment, and announced my personal decision. I am willing to stand behind everything I say, and to accept responsibility for it. In this case, I am standing for what I think is right, for the people or principles I hold dear. When I "stand up" in this way, I am also "standing out" as an autonomous individual. Anyone who stands out is highly visible, sometimes vulnerable, sometimes isolated. Desire for security would counsel me not to take a stand but rather to remain hidden, stay in line, conform, fuse into the anonymous background. Instead of standing out it is easier to "stand by" and watch, be a bystander, a spectator. To stand up for anything takes, literally and metaphorically, a sturdy backbone capable of meeting possible opposition and resistance. Standing up for what one believes and cherishes is commonly considered a mark of autonomous adulthood, of maturity.

Reflection on the colloquial use of words and phrases suggests that standing is a mark of autonomy and independence. The following sections will elaborate and modify this insight as I consider the notion of standing up within such contexts as anthropology, scripture, and theological spirituality.

Called to Stand Erect

Upright posture is first of all an indication of human rather than brute animal life. At the monastery where I live we have Holstein dairy cows. I have sometimes watched with amusement and pity as one of these ponderous beasts rises to its feet from a prone position. On a winter morning after a cow has been lying down all night, its first creaking effort to stand on its feet seems pitifully laborious. The hind limbs are the first to move, lifting the rear as they straighten. At this stage the animal is in a curious posture of supplication, resting on bended front knees. The difficult part of the maneuver follows as nearly a ton of weight is lifted first on one forelimb and then on the other, while the hind hooves dig down for leverage. At last the cow is up, with its weight evenly supported by all four limbs, standing securely and serenely.

Between a quadruped such as the Holstein cow and a biped like the human person, there are vast structural differences. The human infant may crawl on all fours for a number of months until it learns to balance itself in a standing position, but a quadruped will never grow up to be a biped. Between quadrupeds and bipeds are primate animals such as the chimpanzee or orangutan that are capable of balancing themselves for a time on their hind limbs or of walking in a slouched over posture touching the ground with the knuckles of their lengthy forelimbs. These apes are best adapted for life in the trees of the jungle, grasping branches and vines with their flexible feet and hands, feeding on ripe fruit and nuts. Only humans are adapted for habitual upright posture and biped locomotion on the ground.

A principal advantage of erect posture is that the legs suffice for locomotion and the hands are free for making, manipulating, carrying, feeding, gathering and dozens of other functions. A head that is balanced on the spinal column instead of being held by strong muscles permits a larger braincase, reduced jaw, smaller teeth, and pliant lips that aid vocalization. The variable tones of human speech are formed in a resonating chamber left by a larynx that is lower in the throat because of upright posture. Coordinating and utilizing these manifold functions is the work of an expanded and well organized brain. All of these human characteristics are interdependent, but upright posture seems to have a decisive and pivotal importance among them, especially in comparison with nonhuman forms of life.

Whenever anthropologists or archeologists find evidence of upright posture in skeletal remains or fossils, they recognize the signs of human ancestry. A bone from the foot or the leg or the pelvis may be enough from which to deduce the posture, because these bones must be shaped in a certain way to provide attachments for muscles that lift or balance or move the trunk in an erect position. Although human posture is erect, the spinal column is not perfectly straight but somewhat S-shaped, in order to absorb shock, support the head and internal organs, and provide balanced weight distribution. As a result of skeletal and muscle structures that minimize the effect of gravity, standing is a natural, comfortable posture and not fatiguing unless unduly prolonged. Our human anatomy makes standing a distinguishing trait.

The oldest, apparently human footprints discovered thus far were found in petrified volcanic ash at Laetoli, Tanzania, by Dr. Mary Leakey's expedition in 1978. Potassium-argon testing showed an age of around 3.6 million years. Seventy-seven feet of tracks were uncovered, made by two different individuals of small stature. The form of the footprint seems almost modern, with a divergent big toe, a raised arch, a rounded heel. Dr. Mary Leakey believes the individuals who left these tracks stood in the direct line of our human ancestry. Unquestionably they stood fully upright and walked with a free-striding gait. The footprints were not found in a jungle but in what was, as it is today, a grassland or savanna with scattered trees and seed-bearing plants, and an abundance of wildlife that could have sustained a hunting and gathering mode of life.

Dr. Leakey's interpretation of the Laetoli footprints has not yet won complete acceptance because anthropologists are slow to reach agreement on the exact classification of fossil discoveries, especially when it concerns human ancestry. Among the pre-human members of the hominid family are included the extinct genus "erect man" (*homo erectus*), whose limb bones are no different from our own; and the likewise extinct australopithecines, whose limbs are somewhat different and suggest a moderately erect posture and knuckle-walking locomotion. The exact relationship between these pre-humans and humans such as ourselves has not yet been demonstrated to everyone's satisfaction. Are the pre-humans related to us in a direct line of descendance, or are they on a lateral line from some common ancestor? In any case, erect posture seems to be a crucial human development.

If we attempt to gaze upon the entire range of anthropological data from the terrestrial quadrupeds, to the arboreal quadrupeds and bipeds, to the erect terrestrial bipeds culminating in *homo sapiens,* we may discern an upward tendency or dynamism that seems to be drawing living beings toward the fully human stance. This apparent tendency may be described as a call to rise, a call to stand up, a call to move onto a higher level of being. Something of the mystery of being human is reflected in a figure standing still and straight, shoulders back and head held high.

It is possible to speak of this innate call to rise and stand erect without necessarily subscribing to the theory of human evolution. Current theories of human origins, ranging from evolutionism to creationism, face numerous difficulties, and some questions may remain open for a long time to come. The Roman Catholic position allows freedom of investigation as long as there is recognition of the immediate divine creation of the human soul bringing a new, spirit-endowed being into existence. As stated in a 1950 papal encyclical *Humani Generis:*

> The teaching of the Church leaves the doctrine of evolution an open question, as long as it confines its speculations to the development, from other living matter already in existence, of the human body. (That souls are immediately created by God is a view which the Catholic faith imposes on us.)

The foregoing survey of anthropological findings has helped us reflect on the ordinary activity of rising and standing erect. When I made up my mind to go into the kitchen for a cool drink of water and got up from the easy chair I had been resting in, the action of standing up was accomplished gracefully and effortlessly without attending to my upright posture as a sign characteristic of my humanity. Without realizing it, as I got to my feet I was obeying a call not answered so easily by any creature outside the human family. Our reflections on biological history led us to infer a distinctly human or humanizing call to rise and stand erect. The following section will discover a similar call operative in salvation history.

Sacred History in the Old Testament

We do not expect to find in the Old and New Testaments teachings about biology or anthropology that will answer all the questions raised by scientists today. Instead, we find in the Bible a sacred history: the self-revelation of God, a description of the human person, and a record of God's dealings with humanity. The Bible teaches truths about God and the human race that are necessary or helpful for our eternal salvation.

The first three chapters of Genesis propose to be an account of the origin of the cosmos and the human race. In telling the story of Adam and Eve in perhaps the eighth century B.C., the author of Genesis 2–3 (called the Yahwist for his use of that divine name) has left us an account of primeval history that is in some ways also the history of every age and everyman. The Yahwist believed in the radical goodness, greatness, and dignity of human beings as created by Yahweh, but he could not deny the evidence of human frailty and the propensity to evil that he experienced in himself and in society. He believed that human beings were created to live in loving harmony with one another, and yet the reality was often one of hostility, division, rivalry, and manipulation—between the sexes, between individuals, and between nations. The Yahwist also believed that human beings were destined for a beatifying life of familiarity with Yahweh, but he saw people leading lives of futility, frustration, loneliness, and despair, ending in a bleak death. How did things come to be this way? In his reflections on the human situation, the Yahwist was led back to the origins of the human race. In the beginning was set the pattern that has been copied ever since, a pattern of opportunities missed and possibilities unfulfilled, a pattern of sin and salvation.

The Yahwist's narrative opens with a scene in the garden of Eden where there is idyllic harmony between Yahweh, nature, and mankind both male and female. The task assigned to human beings was to cultivate and care for the earth and to assign names to the other creatures, because Yahweh had given humans a share in his power to impose order and have dominion. The only limit to human dominion was that they were not to eat the fruit of the tree of knowledge. Obedience to this commandment was humanity's way of acknowledging its dependent status and basic orientation to the creating God from whose breath it continually drew its life. As long as the commandment was kept, there was an easy familiarity between God and his people, naively suggested by Yahweh's custom of strolling freely about the garden at the breezy time of the day to enjoy the human companionship as well as the evening coolness.

The Yahwist author pictured man and woman in their original condition of innocence as naked yet perfectly able to stand before one another and before their creator, dialoguing without shame or fear. At this point we pick up once again our theme of standing upright. Man and woman stood unclothed but unashamed because they stood in one another's favor and in the favor of their creator. The significance of what it means to be human is hinted at in this primeval ability to rise and stand facing the other in peaceful, free, loving relational and dialogical possibility with full respect for the place each has in the reality of an ordered universe.

The state of original harmony and integrity was disrupted by sin. Humanity lost its innocence through an act of disobedience at the instigation of the tempter who promised, "You will be like gods who know what is good and what is bad" [Gen. 3:5]. That transgression has come to be called "the fall," although the Bible itself does not use this precise term. Instead, the Yahwist left a description of the consequences of the sin: guilt, confusion, fear, and embarrassment before the presence of Yahweh. "The man and his wife hid themselves from the Lord God among the trees of the garden" [Gen. 3:8]. Instead of an unembarrassed stance in openness and confidence before all the world, there is hiding and cowering among the trees, crouching down to avoid being seen. "I was afraid, because I was naked, so I hid myself," said the man in response to Yahweh's summons [Gen. 3:10].

"You will be like gods," the tempter had promised. The motivation underlying the sin was a desire to have absolute dominion and to stand totally independent of Yahweh. The malice of this desire was its prideful assertion of self-sufficiency that turned the first man and woman inward upon themselves in pseudo-independence and presumptuous self-righteousness. Human beings had once been able to stand before Yahweh in dignity and confidence; now they were obliged to hide and to protect themselves from him out of mistrust and suspicion, self-reproach, and shame. Yahweh pronounced his decree of punishment against the tempter, the woman, and the man; finally, he banished them from the garden of Eden and stationed guards to prevent their return.

The Yahwist did not end his story on a completely negative note, however. Humanity may have fallen from an original state of uprightness and integrity, but there remains an orientation towards Yahweh and the hint of final victory after a long struggle: the woman's offspring will crush the serpent's head [Gen. 3:15]. As a touching sign of the steadfast divine protection, Yahweh made leather garments for the man and his wife

to wear in the harsh environment outside the garden [Gen. 3:
21]. Yahweh himself seems to long for the time when he can
once again stroll through the garden with his wayward children
by his side. He did not withdraw his call or invitation for human beings to rise and stand before him, but from now on it
would be up to each individual to stand or fall.

Subsequent history as we read it in Genesis shows a repetition of the pattern that originated with Adam and Eve. On the
one hand there is alienation and disruption, especially in the
social order. Cain was guilty of fratricide. "In the eyes of God
the earth was corrupt and full of lawlessness" [Gen. 6:11]. The
flood came as a divine punishment for lawlessness, but it did
not put an end to the disorder. The episode of the tower of
Babel was another attempt by mankind to "make a name" for
itself and assert its independence, an attempt that ended in ruins
and in dispersion throughout the earth. On the other hand there
are signs in the Genesis narrative of God's constant care for
humanity. He preserved Noah and his family from the flood.
He chose Abraham and blessed him so that he became the father
of a great nation. With that nation God entered into a covenant,
which he kept faithfully in spite of the many instances of in-
gratitude and disobedience on his people's part.

Throughout the long history of Israel's infidelities and re-
forms, there were individuals who answered God's call in an
exceptional way and were permitted to stand before him in a
posture of familiarity and intercession. Such was Moses, who
experienced a revelation of the divinity in a burning bush and
was told: "Remove the sandals from your feet, for the place
where you stand is holy ground" [Exod. 3:5]. Such was Elijah,
who experienced God on Mount Horeb in a tiny whispering
sound: "When he heard this, Elijah hid his face in his cloak and
went and stood at the entrance of the cave" [1 Kings 19:11].
Elijah's successor, Elisha, enjoyed the same relationship: "As
the Lord, the God of Israel, lives, before whom I stand . . . " [2
Kings 3:14]. To stand continually in the house of the Lord, in
his temple at Jerusalem, praising him and praying to him, was
a privilege reserved for his faithful servants [Ps. 135:2]. Ezra,
priest and scribe, feeling the guilt of his people, said: "Because

of all this, we can no longer stand in your presence" [Ezra 9:15]. Ezekiel's prophecy contains a vision promising that the entire nation, now in exile for its sins, would rise from decay and once again stand before God in the promised land. The prophet was shown a field filled with dry bones and told to call them back to life:

> I prophesied as he told me, and the spirit came into them; they came alive and stood upright, a vast army. Then he said to me: Son of man, these bones are the whole house of Israel. . . . Thus says the Lord God: O my people, I will open your graves and have you rise from them, and bring you back to the land of Israel. [Ezek. 37:10–12]

Sacred History in the New Testament

Through Jesus Christ, a new power of rising and standing before God was set loose in a world of frail, fallen human beings. The New Testament was written by people whose faith was built on the resurrection of Jesus from the dead. The Jesus of their experience was the risen Christ now exalted to a place beside the heavenly throne of God where Stephen saw "the Son of Man standing" [Acts 7:56], and where the author of the concluding book of the New Testament saw "a Lamb standing, a Lamb that had been slain" [Rev. 5:6]. The evangelists were conscious of the power emanating from the crucified and exalted Christ and raising all people to a new plane of life: "And I— once I am lifted up from earth—will draw all men to myself" [John 12:32].

Since the evangelists wrote from a post-resurrection perspective, it is not surprising that they should draw attention to the times during the public ministry of Jesus when he physically raised people from sickness and death, and enabled them to stand before him and minister to him or to others. In the opening chapter of Mark's gospel, for example, we have the cure of Peter's mother-in-law: "He went over to her and grasped her hand and raised her, and the fever left her. She immediately began to wait on them" [Mark 1:31]. In the next chapter, a paralytic who had been let down through the roof is commanded: " 'Stand up! Pick up your mat and go home!' The man stood and picked up his mat and went outside in the sight of everyone" [Mark 2:11–12]. Later Jesus expelled a demon, but the afflicted boy was left in a coma: "Jesus took him by the hand and raised him, and he stood up" [Mark 9:27]. On a sabbath, Jesus healed a man who had been sick for thirty-eight years: "Jesus said to him, 'Stand up! Pick up your mat and walk!' The man was immediately cured" [John 5:8]. On two occasions, Jesus brought the dead back to life using the powerful word, "Rise up." The raising of the daughter of Jairus is one instance: "Taking her hand he said to her, *'Talitha, koum,'* which means, 'Little girl, rise.' The girl, a child of twelve, stood up immediately, and began to walk around" [Mark 5:41–42]. The second instance is the raising of the son of the widow of Naim, recorded only by Luke: "He said, 'Young man, I bid you rise.' The dead man sat up and began to speak. Then Jesus gave him back to his mother" [Luke 7:14–15]. Confident of his power, Jesus made a promise to "raise up on the last day" everyone who believed in him [John 6:40], all who stood up for him in this life [John 19:25–26; Luke 21:36].

After the passion and death of Jesus, his chief disciples were empowered by the Spirit of Jesus to carry on his mission of raising people to health and new life. At the Beautiful Gate of the temple, Peter and John restored to a crippled beggar the use of his legs [Acts 3:6–8]. When Peter was questioned about this by the Sanhedrin, he attributed the cure to the name of Jesus: "In the power of that name this man stands before you perfectly sound" [Acts 4:10]. On a visit to Lydda, Peter restored a paralytic named Aeneas who had been bedridden for eight years: "Peter said to him, 'Aeneas, Jesus Christ cures you! Rise and make your bed.' The man stood up at once" [Acts 9:34]. Peter also raised the dead woman Tabitha, using the same word of power Jesus had used: "Turning to the dead body he said, 'Tabitha, stand up.' She opened her eyes, then looked at Peter and sat up. He gave her his hand and helped her to her feet" [Act 9:40–41]. At Lystra, Paul and Barnabas cured a man who was crippled from birth: "Paul called out to him in a loud voice, 'Stand up! On your feet!' The man jumped up and began to walk around" [Acts 14:10]. In the footsteps of Peter, John,

Paul, and Barnabas came a multitude of missionaries spreading the good news of Jesus Christ throughout the known world and helping all people to rise from their sins and recover their dignity as God's children called to stand in his presence [see Rev. 7:9].

The force of renewal and transcendence that began to gain mastery over the powers of disorder and disruption in the world was a force flowing from the resurrection of Christ. On the morning of the third day after Christ's passion and death, Mary Magdalen felt that force by the tomb when something made her turn around and there in the soft sunlight "she caught sight of Jesus standing" [John 20:14]. Paul of Tarsus felt that force not only when a mysterious voice ordered him to "Get up now and stand on your feet" after he had been knocked off his horse [Acts 26:16], but also later when he was held in prison, giving no thought to what lay behind but pushing onward and upward in spirit, straining towards the goal to which he was called: "life on high in Christ Jesus" [Phil. 3:14].

The history of salvation that we have reviewed in these paragraphs seems to culminate in the paschal mystery of Christ's descent into death and his rising again in glory. Humanity, which had stumbled and fallen in Adam and Eve, regained uprightness in Christ. For Christ did not rise alone but "With and in Christ Jesus God raised us up" as well [Eph. 2:6]. The paschal character of human life is manifested in the believers who accept their own fallibility and the limitations of their situation, including their eventual death, because they already possess the hope of a place with the risen Christ in the kingdom of God. The posture of standing before God and the world with limited freedom and regained integrity is a sign of transcendence that already suggests a partial resurrection and anticipates a final transformation [see Col. 3:4]. The call to rise and stand erect that we have traced in salvation history is an orientation to a destiny higher than our unaided nature could ever aspire to, the destiny of standing before God in a free relationship of mutual knowing and loving. The concluding section of this chapter will reflect on this call to rise and stand erect in the context of our ongoing life in the spirit.

Standing Upright in Spirit

In spite of the resurrection and the help of divine grace, the moral life of many of us seems to follow a pattern of falling and getting up again. We are constantly tempted by evil around us and within us, yet constantly called to stand firm in the Lord [1 Thes. 3:8]. The human situation seems as precarious as balancing on a narrow ledge. Overconfidence is a sign of potential disaster. As St. Paul put it, "Let anyone who thinks he is standing upright watch out lest he fall" [1 Cor. 10:12].

Will I stand or fall? That question seems to be the crucial moral issue for life in the spirit, life with God. It is a question that cannot be answered once and for all, but one that faces me day after day. If I have gotten back up on my feet after a fall, will I be able to go on standing securely? If I have fallen, can I hope to ever rise again? Or is it perhaps normal to fall and rise alternately without much stability at either extreme?

From the tradition of the Egyptian desert fathers in the fourth century we have a story that illustrates, in the language of falling and rising, the fluctuation that is a common experience in the moral life:

A brother asked Abba Sisoes, "What shall I do, abba, for I have fallen?" The old man said to him, "Get up again." The brother said, "I have got up again, but I have fallen again." The old man said, "Get up again and again." So then the brother said, "How many times?*

At this point, where the punch line is expected, the story has come down to us in a longer and a shorter version, both of which convey the same teaching. In the shorter version, Abba Sisoes answered the brother in one simple phrase: "Until your death." In the longer version there is an elaboration: "The old man said, 'Until you are taken up either in virtue or in sin. For a man presents himself to judgment in the state in which he is found.'" This version softens the thought of death by speaking of being "taken up" and of "judgment," but it heightens the

---

* Benedicta Ward, trans., *The Sayings of the Desert Fathers,* Cistercian Studies No. 59 (Kalamazoo, Cistercian Publications, 1975), p. 184, no. 38.

ambiguity of the human situation by making it almost a matter of chance whether one dies in the state of sin or of virtue. For our concerns, the point to be stressed is that the spiritual master, Abba Sisoes, was not surprised at his disciple's frequent falls in the moral struggle and advised him not to be discouraged but to keep on getting up again and again with the help of divine grace. In the spiritual life we are like toddlers learning to walk: we may fall repeatedly and take many hard knocks, but someone is usually there to help us up and brush us off; or we manage to get back up again on our own, gaining from the experience and moving beyond it until eventually we learn the trick of keeping our balance and are able to stand with greater confidence. How many times must I fall and rise up? The question is like that put to Jesus by Peter about how often one must forgive a brother who wrongs him. "Seven times?" asked Peter? "No," Jesus replied, "not seven times; I say, seventy times seven times" [Matt. 18:21–22]. The answer proposes an indefinite number and means simply, "As often as necessary." When the willingness is present, the capability will be given.

A twelfth-century Cistercian abbot, St. Bernard of Clairvaux, observed that sometimes we lack the *desire* to stand upright before God, rather than the capability. In his *Sermons on the Song of Songs,* Bernard discussed the verse, "The upright love you" [Song of Sol. 1:3]. He contrasted uprightness with the opposite posture, which he called not fallenness but *curvitas,* a Latin word that implies deliberate slouching, being warped or curved or bent over. Bernard described slouching in his twenty-fourth sermon as a spiritual condition due to seeking and savoring the things of earth; uprightness of spirit, in contrast, is manifest in desiring and reflecting upon the things that are above. Being morally upright or being a slouch depends on the direction that my desires draw me. It is only the upright who love God truly, and love of God is the best exercise for maintaining uprightness. Bernard remarked that human beings are made in the image of God and called by God to cherish uprightness as a mark of spiritual dignity. The upright posture of the body is a constant summons to the human spirit to seek higher rather than lower realities. Bernard used the example of bodily posture quite cleverly when he wrote:

> It is wrong and shameful that this body shaped from the dust of the earth should have its eyes raised on high, scanning the heavens at its pleasure and thrilled by the sight of sun and moon and stars, while, on the contrary, the heavenly and spiritual creature [i.e., the human spirit] lives with its inward vision and affections centered on the earth beneath.*

Bernard pictured an upright body housing a warped spirit that would prefer to dwell on lowly things, like a quadruped walking with downward gaze. Allowing himself to be carried away by his metaphor, Bernard made the body address its own spirit in these reproachful terms:

> Created upright and in your Creator's likeness, you received me as a helper like to yourself, at least in bodily uprightness. . . . You abuse my service to you, a brutish and bestial spirit; you dwell unworthily in this human body.**

From St. Bernard we learn that standing upright in body and spirit is always a possibility, and is the only possibility that does full justice to our humanity created in the image and likeness of God.

Still, the possibility of falling remains as well. And there are times when the distinction between falling and standing is not all that clear. In the vacuum of outer space there is no gravity, no down nor up; astronauts float in their spaceships. I may find myself in a kind of moral vacuum in certain situations or at certain times of life, when for a long period I am not sure whether I am falling or standing firm in spirit. I am not sure which way is up and which way is down. For the present I seem to float weightlessly or coast along, without taking a personal stand. The entertainment industries, the mass media, the advertising agencies, and the government bureaucracy some-

---

* Bernard of Clairvaux, *On the Song of Songs,* trans. Kilian Walsh, Cistercian Fathers No. 7, Sermon 24:II:6 (Kalamazoo: Cistercian Publications, 1976), p. 46.
  ** Ibid.

times contribute to the ambiguity of the situation by imposing standards that discourage people from taking a thoughtful, personal stand. Instead, people are seduced into thinking that everything is gradually getting better, that there is an answer for every problem, that science is just on the verge of a revolutionary breakthrough, that "everybody" is doing this or buying that, or that all governmental decisions may be justified in the name of national security. Tranquilized by such repeated assertions, I can be carried along by the same overpowering wave that sweeps the majority of people through life at a pace that blurs many of the distressing aspects of reality. The wave of progress, it is called, or the wave of the future. But water usually seeks the lowest level, not the highest; it is a cruel illusion to be falling but believe that one is rising. Through no fault of one's own, a long period of life may be passed in such an illusion. Eventually, however, the call to rise and stand erect and free before God will make itself heard in the depths of a sincere heart, for the call is indestructible.

A sincere heart is no proof against a fall but is a promise of a good recovery. A link between sincerity of heart and standing before God has been pointed out by a Russian Orthodox monk and bishop of the nineteenth century, Theophan the Recluse, who wrote: "The principal thing is to stand before God with the mind in the heart, and to go on standing before Him unceasingly day and night until the end of life."* To stand "with the mind in the heart" denotes an attitude of sincerity, attentiveness, centeredness, and integration whereby one's whole being is ordered to the act of prayer or "standing before God." Bishop Theophan's choice of the term *standing* is deeply significant. The prayer he was describing rejoins the converse of Adam and Eve with their creator as they stood before him in their primeval innocence, as well as the prayers of Moses, Elijah, the prophets, and the priests who stood before God [see 2 Macc. 15:12], the prayer of the publican in the gospel parable [Luke 18:10, 13], the prayer of the great white-robed throng

---

* E. Kadloubovsky and E. M. Palmer, trans., *The Art of Prayer: An Orthodox Anthology* (London: Faber and Faber, 1966), p. 63.

standing before the throne of God and of the Lamb [Rev. 7:9], the prayer of the early martyrs and monks, the prayers of those Christians whose images are recorded on the walls of the catacombs standing with hands raised in the orant position. Standing before God with the mind in the heart focuses the totality of one's highest human powers on the divine mystery in whose presence one stands. The posture of standing before God is one of respect as well as intimacy, confident freedom as well as loving fidelity [see 1 John 5:14]. The posture is also one of intercession for others and not simply for oneself. Finally, the upright, standing posture seems appropriate for a prayer of praise, an *Alleluia* or a *Gloria* that rises from deep within the heart and lifts the whole body upward in spirited acclamation or song. In this attitude, Theophan the Recluse would have us "go on standing before Him unceasingly day and night until the end of life."

Conclusion

We have seen how the common, often taken for granted action of rising and standing on one's feet is a marvelously human possibility. Standing up is not only a mark of our humanness in contradistinction to the quadrupeds, it is also a humanizing action that reminds us of our transcendent dignity, and even a reminder of our divinizing call to stand before God. Reflections on the findings of anthropology, on the use of the word "standing" in sacred scripture, and on the development of the metaphor by spiritual masters have opened up for us unexpected perspectives on this ordinary activity. Considered both literally and symbolically, standing up is evidence of the progressive ascent of human beings towards the perfection they are called to attain.

I have contrasted standing up with the experience of falling. There is another symbolic action that does not abrogate the dignity of standing as falling does, but maintains this dignity while putting it entirely at the disposal of another who is considered still higher in dignity. This action, the deep bow, is a convenient thought on which to conclude our considerations.

Only when we have come to appreciate the meaning and the mystery of standing up do we fully appreciate the significance of the deep bow. In the monastery where I live, a deep bow is perhaps our most common liturgical sign of reverence, used instead of a genuflection, and used during the doxology after every psalm chanted at communal prayer services. The deep bow begins from the fully upright, standing position and consists of slowly bending over at the waist. When the bow is made profoundly and reverently, with full attention, it is in itself a form of prayer, silently expressing adoration and surrender. A deep bow is a voluntary act, a conscious placing of myself in a posture of submission before one whom I wish to love and honor.

When I rise and stand erect again after a deep bow, I rise in a new, or renewed, relationship. I regain my former dignity as I stand erect, but now there are new relational bonds that commit me to the one before whom I have bowed. Having freely given myself away to the other in trusting homage, I feel more myself than I was before, more integrated, fulfilled, and completed. In this sense a deep bow may be considered the culmination of our human ability to stand erect. A scene from the book of Revelation borrows the gesture of a deep bow to express the adoration that continues day and night before the heavenly throne of God. The twenty-four elders who represent the totality of God's people are deputed to stand and bow continuously to God: "The twenty-four elders bow down before the One seated on the throne and worship him who lives forever and ever" [Rev. 4:10]. They also chant a song of adoration as they bow, but the words of the song are only an additional articulation of the sentiment already expressed in their deep, ceremonious bow.

SOURCES

"Australopithecus, a Long-Armed, Short-Legged Knuckle-Walker." *Science News* 100 (November 27, 1971).

Encyclopaedia Britannica, 15th ed., Macropaedia, s.v. "Australopithecus"; "Evolution of Man"; "Hominidae"; "Homo Sapiens."

Johanson, Donald C. "Ethiopia Yields First 'Family' of Early Man."
    National Geographic 150, no. 6 (December 1976).
Leakey, Mary D. "Footprints in the Ashes of Time." *National Geo-
    graphic* 155, no. 4 (April 1979).
Morris, Henry M., ed. *Scientific Creationism*. San Diego: Creation-
    Life, 1974.
New Catholic Encyclopedia, s.v. "Human evolution."
Rahner, Karl. "States of Man, Theological." *Sacramentum Mundi,* vol.
    6. New York: Herder and Herder, 1970.

⑥ Eating and Drinking

During the course of our lives we eat thousands of meals. These meals range from simple snacks, when we go into the kitchen for something to munch on and drink, to the formality of a banquet on a special occasion. Again and again we eat, only to become hungry and to eat once more. Mealtime is occasionally postponed or anticipated but is not usually skipped, because hunger and habit bring us back to the table again. For many people, mealtimes are the only fixed and predetermined events in their unpredictable daily schedule.

Because meals are eaten in company with others more often than in solitude, conduct at meals is governed by principles of etiquette and accepted social behavior. After centuries of daily meals, some wise observers of the human situation wrote down for posterity their thoughts and reflections about meals in general. "Better a dish of herbs where love is than a fatted ox and hatred with it," we read in the wisdom literature of the Old Testament [Prov. 15:17]. We find practical advice about temperance and moderation at meals: "If there are many with you at table, be not the first to reach out your hand. Does not a little suffice for a well-bred man? When he lies down, it is without discomfort. Distress and anguish and loss of sleep, and restless tossing for the glutton!" [Sir. 31:18–20]. The sage Qoheleth affirmed the basic goodness of enjoying a meal: "For every man, to eat and drink and enjoy the fruit of his labor is a gift of God" [Eccles. 3:13].

Meals have at times been surrounded by elaborate and even secret rituals, but the process of having a meal is basically quite simple and fundamentally the same in every culture. Food and drink are taken into the mouth and swallowed; all other circumstances are nonessential. However, the other circumstances are important and even of primary importance in particular situations. In this chapter, we will explore the deeper meaning of eating and drinking in order to see how this ordinary experience can put us in touch with the mystery of life and the mystery of a nurturing God. Our reflections on meals will eventually lead us to the New Testament texts concerning the sacred meal of the Eucharist and the joyful sharing of the great feast in the kingdom of God.

A Family Meal in Nepal

In November of 1973, Peter Matthiessen was returning to civilization from a trek in the Tibetan plateau on a quest for the Himalayan snow leopard. By nightfall he had reached the village of Rohagaon in Nepal, built on a mountainside at an elevation close to ten thousand feet, overlooking the deep gorge of the Suli Gad River. Although he was unable to speak the language, Matthiessen begged hospitality from a villager who was apparently afflicted with an eye disease. "Infected Eye," as Matthiessen calls the man in his journal, accepted a rupee note in payment, then cooked and served eggs to his guest before he and his own family had their meal. Later, Matthiessen watched in silent fascination from his place on a goatskin near the family hearth as the wife of Infected Eye prepared their own evening meal. She was efficient and careful in her movements, confident in her ability to manage the small fire, the simple utensils, the few items of food. Matthiessen felt that he was in the presence of an ancient, almost sacred ritual:

> The slow deft handling of burning twigs as *tsampa* and dried pumpkin squash are cooked on a brazier, the breadmaking, the murmuring, the love and food extended to the children without wasted words or motion, the tenderness toward the sick husband—all has the pace and dignity of a sacrament.*

When Infected Eye had finished his meal, his wife and children helped him recline against the earthen wall, tucked blankets

---

* Peter Matthiessen, *The Snow Leopard* (New York: Bantam, 1978), p. 304.

around him and laid the infant in beside him. Only then did the wife have a bite to eat—her children's leavings—before she put away the cooking utensils, sighed, yawned, spread a mat on the dirt floor, and lay down beside her husband.

In other huts in the village a similar scene was taking place as it had taken place at mealtime every day in the lives of the people of Rohagaon. Special occasions in the history of the family or the village were celebrated with greater festivity and communal sharing, but such occasions were infrequent. Mealtime in Rohagaon would differ in many ways from the ordinary evening meal of a family in developed countries, but the basic structure of preparing and eating a meal together would be virtually the same. Peter Matthiessen, without understanding the spoken language, understood the universal language of an evening meal and felt part of the scene as an honored guest at the family hearth. The primitive simplicity and dignity of the meal made him think of a sacred ritual, or reminded him of a sacral dimension of experience present in all fully human mealtime situations.

Feeding, Eating, Dining

There are various ways of being nourished, as exemplified by three forms of eating and drinking: the primary activity of feeding, the ordinary experience of eating a meal, and the special occasions of dining or feasting. Food nourishes life, but as a human being I live on several different planes.

Feeding activity.   First of all I must take in enough food to maintain my energy, health, and physical life processes. I share this feeding activity with all the animals. When I am extremely hungry I might say that I want to "put on the feed bag," like a horse. If I am actually starving to death I will feed compulsively on any available food.

When consuming the food is the paramount concern, the niceties of conversation and table manners are forgotten. Feeding is largely a solitary activity and resists social interaction. Meals eaten alone can degenerate to the level of mere feeding, like an animal; but even in the presence of others one's participation in a meal may be reduced to feeding activity if the others are ignored and attention is focused entirely on the food. Wolfing one's food or gorging oneself or eating mechanically without knowing what is being eaten—all these tend to be simply feeding activity. Although it is a consequence of natural physical need, feeding seems to be a less than fully human form of having a meal.

Eating a meal.   In the common experience of eating a meal, physical nourishment is not the only concern as it is in the case of feeding. Perhaps the majority of Americans are accustomed to eating three times a day, not because three square meals are necessary to ward off starvation but because this is a social custom. We look forward to mealtime not only for the pleasure of good food but also for reasons connected with meeting other people or with the rhythm of working and resting or with events that go on simultaneously with the meal.

As we eat a meal, usually in company with others but sometimes alone, we nourish the body with food and drink, but we are also nourished on a higher level of the self, mentally or aesthetically or emotionally, by the relationships at play during the meal. Table talk is a characteristic feature of a shared meal. Even without conversation there may be a relationship of sharing and of fellowship, as at the common meal in a monastery dining room where, instead of conversing, it is customary to listen to edifying or entertaining readings.

When people wish to show hospitality to a guest or to celebrate a special occasion such as a birthday, wedding, or family reunion, they eat a meal together. In these cases, the principal reason for a meal is not physical nourishment but the atmosphere of joy and conviviality generated by eating and drinking at a common table. Because our humanness transcends the animal level of feeding, the experience of eating a meal can carry many meanings. Eating together signifies and promotes fellowship, harmony, reconciliation and the celebration of life. A family picnic at the park or a cookout in the back yard heightens the feeling of being a family. Meetings of social groups and clubs often begin or conclude with a meal to strengthen the bonds of group solidarity. Bonding is further strengthened if the group voluntarily restricts its diet, as by abstaining from meat or certain beverages.

Dining.   Feasting or dining is a special modality of eating a meal. I recall a comment someone made as a group was clearing dishes from the table after a meal that had lasted about forty minutes longer than usual and had been marked by more hilarity and more profundity of conversation than usual. This person's comment was: "The other nights we ate together, but tonight we can say that we dined." The good food was no different from usual, but some other chemistry was in the air to make the interaction at the dining table greatly satisfying for all. People were nourished on deeper levels of the self at that meal. Just as feeding primarily nourishes the body, and eating a meal together nourishes the social-relational level of the self, dining means nourishment for the human spirit.

We eat every day; but a meal that feasts the spirit is not a frequent occurrence. We survive from feastday to feastday, storing up in our spirit the sense of meaningfulness and hope that is renewed each time we dine. A feast is different from the superficiality of a cocktail party, where only a frothy euphoria is permitted. Feasting, or dining, implies and fosters the honest sharing of the experience of life in its complexity. Dining does not take place in solitude but always with at least one other to share with and reveal oneself to. The food that is eaten at a memorable dinner is not always remembered as clearly as the mutual sharing and self-disclosure that took place. But the food can of course contribute to the festive atmosphere by its abundance and variety, its attentive preparation and its appeal to the palate. The special magic of a feast cannot be evoked at will, but an atmosphere may be deliberately designed in which the experience of dining is more likely to happen. Dining raises the ordinary experience of eating and drinking to its perfection.

The Meaning of Meals

Eating a meal is first of all an assertion of my will to live and to be what I am. A dying person who has lost the will to live loses his or her appetite as well. If I am sick and not feeling like myself, I cannot do justice to a meal. The opposite extreme—overeating—may express a hunger for more than food, and may be the vehicle of numerous meanings depending on the individual's life history and situation. Food typifies us; but it is not only the quantity and quality of what we eat, but how and why we eat that makes us be as we are.

Eating and drinking happen again and again. Even the most satisfying meal only satisfies temporarily. People always get hungry again. What is the meaning of this repetitiousness of meals? Food sustains life, and life is constantly slipping away like sand through an hourglass. No one has a permanent hold on life, because we do not give life to ourselves. Life is given to us as a pure gift from a divine source of superabundant, over-brimming vitality. Having to eat again and again reminds me that life and the food that sustains life are ultimately God's gift, and not something I can secure for myself once and for all. The starving poor are perhaps the ones who appreciate this fact, and appreciate mealtime, more readily than others.

Since food sustains the gift of life, sharing a meal with others speaks of fellowship in shared life. Without actually saying it in so many words, my willingness or unwillingness to eat with another communicates acceptance or rejection of fellowship with that person. To share the same table and perhaps the same food is to share life. Refusal to join another for a meal means that we do not have that much in common right now. By preference, I eat with my friends or with those I wish to know as friends. The common table presupposes, or brings about, equality for a time. Agreements are often sealed or celebrated with a meal because of the natural bonding that occurs among table companions. In the Old Testament, covenants or peace treaties were ratified by a shared meal, as when Joshua made a covenant with the Gibeonites without knowing they were from a nearby town [Josh. 9:14–15]. The covenant between God and his chosen people was ratified with a meal on Mount Sinai, when Moses and the seventy elders beheld the God of Israel and ate a meal in his presence without harm: "After gazing on God, they could still eat and drink" [Exod. 24:11].

In probably every culture and period of history, a shared meal has symbolized solidarity, peace, mutual trust, and joyful friendliness. If fellow-feeling and concord are absent, or if it seems more prudent to be cautious, individuals and groups will prefer to eat separately (for a biblical example, see Gen. 43:32). Religious ritual customs for meals or family mealtime customs strengthen bonds of cohesiveness among members of the group. At Metropolitan Stadium in suburban Minneapolis, as at other stadia, the custom of "tailgating" has created a festive spirit of community after football games, especially when the home team has been victorious. Tailgates of the station wagons come down and there are picnics in the parking lot, including barbecue-grilled steaks and background music, as the traffic thins out. A shared meal is a celebration of shared life.

Van Gogh's Potato Eaters

Nineteenth-century impressionist Vincent van Gogh sympathized and identified most with common folk, peasant farmers and laborers, neglected people, the disadvantaged. In their patient acceptance of their lot, Vincent sensed a deep vein of integrity and wisdom, a kind of saintliness. Vincent's large oil painting of the *Potato Eaters,* completed in Holland in the spring of 1885, reflects his heartfelt feelings about the laborious life of country people. "The painting speaks of manual labor," Vincent wrote to his brother in a letter on April 30th, "and tells that they have earned their keep so honestly." In Vincent's own judgment, this painting was "the best one" of his early works.

The scene is the evening meal, under the orange light of an oil lamp that leaves mysterious shadows in the small, crude cottage. A steaming platter of potato chunks rests on the rough wooden table. At the corner of the table four coffee cups are being carefully filled by the mother of the family, while her grey-haired husband holds a fifth cup for her. At the opposite corner of the table two young adults, a man with a protruding muzzle and a woman with large, beseeching eyes, are spearing potatoes with their forks. The meal is just beginning. The fifth figure is central in the painting, but the viewer sees only her back and must imagine her to be the younger daughter. All wear bonnets or visored caps, as if they had just come in from a day in the fields. Their hands, which are as gnarled as tree knots, have turned the soil for planting, pulled the weeds, picked bugs from the leaves, have dug, washed, and peeled those potatoes, and are now holding the final fruit of their toil. The scene is primitive but noble. The evident poverty has not been allowed to diminish human dignity. No smiles or small talk can be detected, but only a serene, silent earnestness and reverence.

This family of potato eaters has gathered to share the only food they have to sustain their existence. The symbolism of eating and drinking as a sharing of life comes through strongly as these laborers help themselves to their potatoes from a common dish. The intensity of the moment suggests a sacred ritual, a kind of sacrament. Vincent has omitted all traditional religious symbols (with the possible exception of a calvary tableau in a picture on the wall of the cottage), but the meal that binds this family together is religious in its basic humanness and simplicity. If one were to look at the painting for parallels with the Christian sacrament, one could point to the lamp that glows like a candle, the table that is like an altar, the potatoes and coffee that are like the elements of bread and wine, and the gesture of the father of the family reverently holding a cup as if he were elevating a chalice. Such parallels are not likely to have been present to the artist's mind, although Vincent once made an attempt to follow the vocation of an evangelist. The *Potato Eaters* has a religious and eternal quality because its subject matter is the mystery of life shared at a common meal.

The Mystery Obscured

If our common meals often lack the dimension of sacredness and mystery, perhaps it is because we have allowed the mystery to be crowded out by functionality, haste, or routine. Busy schedules often make it difficult to choose a time when all can be present for a meal; when someone is missing, the loss of that person's contribution to the meal diminishes the effect of the experience for all. The effect the experience of eating and drinking together should have is also lost when mealtime becomes wartime and the conversation is electric with anger, recrimination, harsh teasing, or nagging. Not uncommonly, the desire for an efficient use of time leads to doing several things at once: eating while reading mail, eating while watching television, eating while driving to the next appointment. In such circumstances, the meal loses most of its effectiveness except on the level of physical nourishment,

Even the bare minimum of physical nourishment is in jeopardy when haste reduces mealtime to "grabbing a bite to eat." Indigestion, constipation, and stomach ulcers may eventually be the price paid for these "eat and run" meals. The current trend, judged by the rising profits of American food service industries, is to eat outside the home and to eat fast. Rushing through a meal is only one instance of the rapid pace of living in our contemporary culture. Technology has speeded up our ability to accomplish tasks, so that we are driven to accomplish more tasks, driven to live at a faster rate. Haste tyrannizes our lives and empties them of experiences that need to be savored slowly to be appreciated, like a meal. Haste takes away our freedom to savor, to dwell, to enjoy, to wonder. Ultimately, haste dehumanizes us and remakes us according to the model of a machine. Food is pulled from a dispensing machine and stuffed into a human digesting machine with barely enough time in between to remove the plastic wrapper. Then meals are devoid of mystery.

Sensitivity to Mystery

To appreciate the meaning of eating and drinking and to open myself to the mystery of being nourished in my total humanity, I might begin by slowing down. When I have resolved to take my time, I can develop attentiveness to the experience of eating and drinking. I can slowly become aware of texture, color, nuances of taste, aware of chewing and swallowing; and then I can extend my awareness to the table, the room, the people who may be sharing the meal with me, and the demands of the current topic of conversation. Although it may seem strange at first, slowing one's pace during mealtime is not artificial nor unnatural, but in perfect harmony with the process of digestion and the tempo of relaxed table talk. If a family or a group occasionally chooses to eat a meal in comfortable silence, the atmosphere of calmness can facilitate awareness and appreciation of the meaning of eating and being nourished.

In an unpublished master's thesis on the theme of "Spiritual Awakening and a Sense of Wonder," Mary Mester has described an experience of pausing for a moment during a silent meal and gazing attentively at a half-circle of teethmarks left in the heavily buttered slice of homemade bread she held in her hand. Then she became aware of the piece of bread that had been in that half-circle of space and was now in her mouth. Slowly and consciously she resumed chewing that piece of coarsely textured bread, savoring the whole-grain taste and the honey-sweetened butter. She thought of all that had gone into making that slice of bread: the wheat sown, harvested, and ground to flour; the flour kneaded into yeasted dough and baked. She thought of the butter mixed with honey, thanks to the cows with their creamy milk and to the bees searching for nectar. As she enjoyed this simple food, Mary Mester surrendered to the gentle mystery of being nourished and sustained in life. Spontaneously, she felt grateful: "I was glad, quietly but deeply glad, for sun and soil; for grain and rain; sowers, bakers, and table-setters; for bread that lets itself be eaten . . . and for Life, perpetuating all this in its fecundity."

Slowing down to eat can increase my sensitivity to this basic experience of being nourished in life. Eating and drinking take place in peaceful harmony with life and all that accompanies it in the daily turning of the earth and the yearly cycle of the seasons. The nutrients I absorb from food are used and then given back to the earth from which they came. The eater and the eaten merge and then diverge in the stream of life that carries and sustains us all. This stream of life has a divine source. When people are gratefully aware of that divine source, the mystery of the ordinary is revealed in eating and drinking.

Children of a Nourishing God

The psalmist was conscious of life and food as coming from God when he wrote:

> You raise grass for the cattle, and vegetation for men's use,
> Producing bread from the earth, and wine to gladden men's hearts. . . .
> They all look to you to give them food in due time.
> When you give it to them, they gather it,
> When you open your hand, they are filled with good things. [Ps. 104:14–15; 27–28]

The divine gift of life is given with a generous hand, because God's nature is a love that nourishes and sustains without counting the cost. The nature of God as caring, nurturing, and parental is revealed in the mystery of our daily food and drink.

Because the biblical people of God realized that their daily food was the gift of a nurturing creator to his needy children, they always began their meals by blessing God for his loving kindness. In a typical form, this blessing ran: "Blessed are you, O Lord our God, King of the world, who bring forth bread from the earth." In the setting of a family meal, the right to say the blessing belonged to the father of the family while the other members responded "Amen." The grace before meals was never omitted, even by someone eating alone. God's power as Lord and King of creation had to be acknowledged and thanked before his gifts could be enjoyed. To partake of the food over which a blessing had been said was to share in the blessing and to be nourished in the life that is God's primary gift to his children. The blessing said over the food was also an implicit invitation to the Lord and King to favor this shared meal with his presence. Meals had a religious character because the blessing invoked the presence of God at the table. Orthodox Israelite customs did not imitate pagan cultures, which thought that oblations of food and drink were actually consumed by the deity (illustrated by the story of Bel and the Dragon in Dan. 14). But the rites in the temple of Jerusalem did include libations, show-bread, and other food offerings which were reserved for the meals of the priests [Exod. 29:41; Lev. 24:5–9; 23:20].

God nourishes his people not only with physical food but also with his word of life, which is the source of true happiness. A touching example where both forms of nourishment are offered occurs in the life of Elijah when he fled into the desert to escape the wrath of Queen Jezebel [1 Kings 19:1–18]. God sent his angel to feed Elijah with a hearth cake and a jug of water so that he would have strength to walk to Horeb, the mountain of God. There God's word came to Elijah in the whisper of a gentle breeze and told him what to do and where to go next. "Not by bread alone does man live, but by every word that comes forth from the mouth of God" [Deut. 8:3; Matt. 4:4]. Not to know God's will causes more anguish than the lack of bread, as the prophecy of Amos puts it: "Yes, days are coming, says the Lord God, when I will send famine upon the land; not a famine of bread, or thirst for water, but for hearing the word of the Lord" [Amos 8:11]. God's silence was his final mode of punishing a disobedient and hardhearted people. Most of the time there was no famine of the word of God because the prophets communicated God's will to the people, after being nourished by it themselves. Ezekiel, for instance, was given a scroll to eat that was sweet as honey in his mouth, and was then sent forth to speak the words he had assimilated [Ezek. 3:1–4].

When God nurtures the life of his people with food and drink and with the consolation of his word, he is lavish with these gifts. His people were thirsty as they crossed the desert to the promised land, so God commanded Moses to strike the rock with his staff, and water gushed forth like a stream [Ps. 105:41]. His people were hungry, and he nourished them with a daily supply of manna that fell upon the camp like dew and tasted like honeyed wafers [Exod. 16:14–31]. His people longed for meat, and God summoned a wind that drove in quail from the sea "and brought them down over the camp site at a height of two cubits from the ground for the distance of a day's journey all around the camp" [Num. 11:31]. Generosity without limit! In the time of the prophet Elisha, a widow's jug of oil was able to fill as many vessels as she could borrow from all her neighbors [2 Kings 4:1–7], and twenty barley loaves were set before a hundred men who ate their fill and had some left over [1 Kings 4:42–44].

The New Testament continues the story of the divine extravagance. At the beginning of his ministry of liberation and liberality, Jesus changed about a hundred gallons of water into wine for a wedding feast at Cana in Galilee [John 2:6–9]. Jesus taught his disciples to pray confidently for their daily bread [Matt. 6:11], and he himself demonstrated the superabundant effects of such trust when he multiplied five loaves among five thousand, and seven loaves among four thousand [Matt. 16:9–10]. Afterwards, there were baskets and baskets full of leftovers. The doublet form of these accounts serves to underline the astonishing prodigality of God's gifts in the Messianic age.

A special feature of the Messianic lavishness is that no one is excluded from these meals unless he chooses to exclude himself. All are invited to the feast, without discrimination [Luke 14:15–24]. Jewish expectation was that the kingdom of God would be restricted to those who had accepted the Torah with its dietary and ritual customs, including circumcision. Jesus announced a more universal policy: "Mark what I say! Many will come from the east and the west and will find a place at the banquet in the kingdom of God with Abraham, Isaac, and Jacob" [Matt. 8:11]. Not only in words did Jesus announce this good news, but also by his own actions. He excluded no one from his table fellowship: "The tax collectors and sinners were all gathering around to hear him, at which the Pharisees and the scribes murmured, 'This man welcomes sinners and eats with them' " [Luke 15:1]. Jesus accepted a drink of water from a Samaritan woman [John 4:7–9], and accepted invitations to dine with tax collectors [Mark 2:15; Luke 19:7]. These practices earned Jesus the scorn of those who feared defilement from eating with sinners: "This is a glutton and drunkard, a lover of tax collectors and those outside the law" [Matt. 11:19]. But it was the mission of Jesus to call sinners [Mark 2:17] and to show them God's forgiveness by sharing a meal with them. Table companionship symbolizes acceptance, reconcilation, peace (see, for example, 2 Kings 25: 27–30, and John 21:12–13, where the risen Christ eats with the disciples who had previously forsaken him).

Eucharist and Agape

Jesus must have shared many more meals with his disciples than are recorded in the New Testament. These daily meals, whether in the company of a large crowd or the intimacy of the twelve, and whether eaten out of doors or in homes where hospitality was offered, brought into being an intimate fellowship around the person of Jesus. The passover supper that was Jesus' final meal with his disciples before his passion transformed that fellowship group into the redeemed community of the new age opened by the death and exaltation of Jesus. These faithful followers who ate the torn bread that Jesus had made his body and drank from the cup of wine that he had made his blood became the representatives of God's new people, a people forgiven, sanctified, and nourished with divine life [1 Cor. 10: 16–17]. They are the first of those "many" on whose behalf Jesus poured out his life as he sealed a new covenant with humanity [Mark 14:24; Matt. 20:28].

In the bread and wine of the last supper, Jesus made a complete gift of himself to others—"for you" [Luke 22:19; 1 Cor. 11:24]. Here is the food that gives life to the world, God's bread that comes down from heaven to nourish his hungry children [John 6:32–33]. In this sacramental rite, ordinary bread becomes the living bread: "The bread I will give is my flesh, for the life of the world" [John 6:51]. The faithful who gather to renew the Lord's supper in remembrance of Jesus are united in mysterious fellowship with him: "He who feeds on my flesh and drinks my blood has life eternal" [John 6:54].

Life eternal is divine life, the life of all who will have a place in the kingdom of God and partake of the heavenly banquet. The Eucharistic meal already anticipates and prefigures this banquet of the final age. Jesus said to those who had shared his last supper: "You are the ones who have stood loyally by me in my temptations. . . . In my kingdom you will eat and drink at my table" [Luke 22:28–30]. The bread and wine of the Eucharist are not given in quantities that satisfy physical hunger, because they are a foretaste of the feast at the end of time that will satiate every hunger of the human heart [Luke 6:20]. There the longing for an experience of intimately shared life will be fulfilled: "If anyone hears me calling and opens the door, I will enter his house and have supper with him, and he with me" [Rev. 3:20; see Luke 12:37]. There the longing for perfect fellowship will be complete in the joyful union of a marriage banquet: "Happy are they who have been invited to the wedding feast of the Lamb" [Rev. 19:9]. To sustain their hope and hunger for the final return of their Lord, Christians have habitually gathered for the breaking of bread and the blessing of the cup "until he comes" [1 Cor. 11:26; see the petition for his coming 16:22; Rev. 22:20].

The meals shared at the gathering of Christians in the years immediately after the resurrection of Christ continued the table fellowship of Jesus and his disciples that began during the public ministry and culminated in the last supper: "They devoted themselves to the apostles' instruction and the communal life, to the breaking of bread and the prayers" [Acts 2:42]. These fellowship meals, where believers "partake of the table of the Lord" [1 Cor. 10:21] in a mysterious experience of his presence, were held "in their homes" [Acts 2:40], or in rooms suitable for larger groups ["an upstairs room," Acts 20:8]. These fraternal gatherings took place at evening "on the first day of the week" and perhaps more frequently [Acts 20:7].

By the early second century, the fellowship meals held in remembrance of the Lord came to be called Eucharists, from a Greek word implying praise and thanks [see Mark 14:23; Col. 4:2]. The Eucharist as the ritual remembrance of the Lord's Supper can be differentiated from the Agape, or love feast, that often accompanied the Eucharist, either preceding or following it. Food supplied by more fortunate Christians was eaten by the poor and by widows at the Agape in fulfillment of Christ's commands to show charity towards the needy [Luke 14:12–14]. But whenever free food and drink are available, abuses are possible. The letter of Jude admits that there were disturbances in the Agapes: "These men are blemishes on your love feasts, as they boldly carouse together, looking after themselves" [Jude 12, RSV]. Perhaps the classic example is the description of the meals of the Christians in Corinth [1 Cor. 11:17–34]. Paul accused them of quarreling, drunkenness, shaming the poor, and eating their own supper without waiting for one another. Because of such abuses and because of the desire to receive the Eucharist fasting, the Agape was separated from the Eucharist and held in the evening, while the Eucharist was celebrated in the morning, at least around the mid-second century. Over the next few centuries, the Agape meal gradually disappeared as other forms of assistance to the needy developed. Perhaps in the contemporary custom of sometimes staying to socialize over coffee and rolls after a festive Eucharist we may see a revival of the Agape meal in a new form.

With Exultant Hearts

About the early Christians we read: "With exultant and sincere hearts they took their meals in common" [Acts 2:46]. The typical mood that prevailed at the common meal was joy and gladness, whether that meal was an Agape or a Eucharist or an integration of both. Festal joy was a spontaneous response to the bonds of fellowship, to the mysterious presence of the Spirit of the Lord and to the assurance of salvation and forgiveness that they experienced in faith [see Acts 16:34].

Eating and drinking are a natural source of joy in themselves. A shared meal is already a sufficient occasion for delight, because food is generally something that can be appreciated and enjoyed by all, including especially the poor. "Go, eat your bread with joy and drink your wine with a merry heart," was the homey advice given by the sage Qoheleth [Eccles. 9:7]. Mealtime should be a time of good cheer, ranging from a feeling of quiet satisfaction to expressions of unrestrained jubilation, depending on the occasion, the company, and the cuisine.

The natural joy of a pleasant meal became a biblical symbol for the perfect happiness of the kingdom of God. The bliss of the kingdom burst forth already in the table fellowship of Jesus and his companions. Jesus was no ascetic like John the Baptist, who stressed the appropriateness of fasting and compunction. John's disciples were scandalized to see Jesus and his companions enjoying themselves at banquets. Jesus answered them: "How can the wedding guests go in mourning so long as the groom is with them?" [Matt. 9:15]. Joy at the nearness of the kingdom is characteristic also of the Christian Eucharist, as we have seen. The perfect joy of the kingdom itself is described as a lavish banquet of rich food and choice wines [Prov. 9:1–5]. There the guests will taste the "new wine" that gladdens the heart [Matt. 26:29; Ps. 104:15; John 2:10). Their beatitude will be the nuptial joy of the divine wedding feast. This promise was written down for a permanent record at the command of an angel: "The angel then said to me: 'Write this down: Happy are they who have been invited to the wedding feast of the Lamb!' " [Rev. 19:9]. The happiness of our present meals is only the first course of an eternal banquet in the kingdom of God and of the Lamb.

Conclusion

It is possible that we have repeated the ordinary experience of eating and drinking thousands of times without a thought for the process itself and for its deeper levels of meaning as a mystery of nourishment, fellowship, and celebration of life. When we began to reflect on mealtime experience as described by Peter Matthiessen in Nepal and by Vincent van Gogh in his painting of the *Potato Eaters,* we caught the sense of something sacred in the sharing of food. To share food is to share life with others, both life and food being divine gifts. Thus meals are a natural symbol for fellowship and friendliness, mutual peace and trust. Meals celebrate life at its most reliable and hopeful level.

The mystery of life is touched at mealtime unless routine or haste or a purely functional approach crowds it out. We reflected on the potential benefit of slowing down for meals in order to let awareness and appreciation deepen, not to mention the improvement of digestion. Slowing down to be nourished can open one's awareness to the ultimate source of nourishment: a nurturing and mothering God. The Old and the New Testaments both record God's lavish gifts for the nourishment of the people. We saw how the history of divine nourishment culminates in the mystery of the Eucharist, the living bread. Sharing a meal at the table of the Lord with the community of the redeemed is a heightened experience of eating and drinking together in the context of ordinary daily life. The sacred meal is the exemplar of all others, or all other meals are sacred because they somehow reflect the sublime experience of the table of the Lord where humans share life with a nurturing God. A spirit of festal joy brightens the meals of all who can perceive the mysteries present in the ordinary experience of eating and drinking.

SOURCES

Daniélou, Jean. *The Bible and the Liturgy.* Notre Dame: University of Notre Dame Press, 1956.

Edwards, Tilden. *Living Simply Through the Day.* New York: Paulist, 1977.

Jeremias, Joachim. *The Eucharistic Words of Jesus,* trans. Norman Perrin. Philadelphia: Fortress, 1977.

Léon-Dufour, Xavier, ed. *Dictionary of Biblical Theology.* 2d rev. ed., s.v. "Meal." New York: Seabury Press, 1973.

Mester, Sr. Mary, R.S.M. *Spiritual Awakening and A Sense of Wonder.* Unpublished master's thesis, Center for the Study of Spirituality, Institute of Man, Duquesne University, Pittsburgh, 1975.

New Catholic Encyclopedia, s.v. "Agape" by Casimir Bernas; "Eucharist (Biblical Data)" by Casimir Bernas; "Meal, sacred" by Caroll Stuhlmueller.

Verhoeven, Cornelis. *The Philosophy of Wonder,* trans. Mary Foran. New York: Macmillan, 1971.

7 Hurting

Life is prodigal with its beauty, its blessings, and its joys, but to everyone it deals out a liberal share of hurts as well. Discovering the mystery of the ordinary is sometimes a matter of discerning the deepest source of both the goodness and the harshness of life, and discerning the place of both in the divine plan. One day when Jesus was telling his followers to act more like their heavenly Father, he said: "His sun rises on the bad and the good, he rains on the just and the unjust" [Matt. 5:45]. Both the sunshine of comfort and joy, and the rain of hurts and afflictions fall without discrimination upon rich and poor, black and white, young and old alike. I have no choice about the weather bringing me sunshine or rain, or about life bringing me hard knocks or soothing strokes. I learn to enjoy the strokes as they come, and to take my knocks when I get them. This chapter deals with the knocks and hurts, because these, apparently devoid of meaning, benefit, mystery, are often hardest to take.

Throughout this chapter I adopt a biblical and Christian perspective. I believe that the mystery of Christ crucified and seemingly abandoned by his Father best illuminates the mystery of human suffering, and suggests how God can still be found and loved in the midst of pain, unpleasantness of every kind, sadness and loneliness, misunderstanding, bone-wearying toil, or battering and violence. As a child I put band-aids on my cuts, bumps, and bruises (as well as on broken toys and cracks in the wall). As an adult I try, with much less success, to heal my wounded ego or hurt feelings by hiding them beneath the bandage of a smiling, pleasant countenance. Exteriorly and physically I can appear serene, while inside I am bleeding to death from insults, heartaches, emotional or spiritual anguish, or from being neglected, ignored, or tormented by those from whom I have a right to expect more consideration. Even in these situations, the mystery of the crucified Christ forgiving his enemies from the cross suggests a possibility of rising above my hidden hurts and opening my life to the healing power of the resurrection.

Simone Weil, who knew much about affliction and much about the mystery of Christ, although she never accepted baptism, maintained in her book *Gravity and Grace* that "the extreme greatness of Christianity lies in the fact that it does not seek a supernatural remedy for suffering but a supernatural use for it." The immediate supernatural usefulness of affliction is to teach me how poor, vulnerable, needy, naked, and fragile I really am. I imagine I am something, whereas in fact I am nothing [see Gal. 6:3]. Without suffering I would go on living in the complacent illusion of having it all together and being on top of it all, through skillful management and superior preparation. The hurt that shatters that illusion is useful because it collapses the house of cards my ego has painstakingly erected and carefully held in balance. The shock of being badly hurt is enough to bring the whole structure down on my head and leave me exposed to the sun, the rain, and the wind.

Suffering in itself is not good, but can be turned to good use. It hurts to get hurt, but there may be no better way to puncture my false sense of well-being and expose me as I am in truth. The feeling of exposure is uncomfortable, but it is preferable to being imprisoned in an illusion about my true condition. The pain that washes over me liberates and leaves me capable of savoring life afresh. "Blest are you poor," said Jesus [Luke 6: 20]. Blest are all who are open to the truth about themselves, open to others in compassion, and lovingly open to life in all its mystery. They are blessed because they are heirs to a kingdom of "peace and justice" [Heb. 12:11].

Coping with the Fog

Last winter for six weeks during December and January we had fog nearly all day every day. The weather bureau had a scientific explanation for it, but this did not help lift people's spirits. The succession of cold, dreary days grated on the nerves and increased irritability. People became depressed, grouchy, petty, impatient. Traffic accidents soared. Airline flights were canceled. Getting sick seemed the sensible thing to do under the circumstances. The monastery where I live receives all year around a steady trickle of requests for prayers in desperate cases. During the fog, the trickle of requests became a stream of letters and phone calls. There were numerous deaths and cases of cancer, heart attacks, alcoholism, and injuries to pray for. It was as if the fog had become a blanket of misery.

Christmas and New Year seemed less festive than usual last winter because of the unrelenting fog and misery. Christmastime is often a stressful season for people, especially if their own feelings are not in tune with the glittering, rejoicing images presented on every side by high-powered advertisements. Those who cannot afford lavish gifts and entertainments feel left out. When people cannot meet expectations laid on them by others or even by themselves, they feel like failures. January is the peak month for attempted and accomplished suicides. Mental health clinics in our area were pushed to the limit trying to help people who became discouraged during the long winter fog.

When the fog lifted and the sun shone again in a blue sky, as it had to eventually, people took deep breaths of the cool, pure air and began to smile once more. We silently congratulated ourselves on having somehow muddled through the crisis. In fact, we had done very little but endure the pain of it, more or less gracefully, until it passed away by itself. Some of life's hurts do pass away of their own accord, and the easiest way to handle them is to wait them out patiently. To imagine that everything should always be pleasurable and beautiful in life, as the advertising media would convince us, is to indulge in an unrealistic fantasy that will one day crumble under misfortune's blows. But fortune can in turn replace misfortune if we expect it and if we believe strongly enough in the power of divine love to arrange all things for the ultimate benefit of those who have been called [Rom. 8:28]. In the perspective of a long-term view, we have the assurance that "eye has not seen, ear has not heard, nor has it so much as dawned on man what God has prepared for those who love him" [1 Cor. 2:9].

Our own bodies have remarkable powers of self-healing to enable us to make complete recoveries from many injuries, ill-nesses, and surgical interventions. Time and cooperation with the body's natural efforts gradually heal our physical hurts. Even in the area of mental illness, if healing occurs it is some-times because the infraconscious resources of the mind have been released with the help of a therapist so that a natural func-tional balance is restored. The healing process accelerates in a climate of human dignity and love.

The family is the natural milieu for healing many of life's hurts, especially those inflicted outside the home in the world of business, politics, and social services. Dealing with other people in our competitive society can sometimes be like trying to swim with barracudas. Sooner or later someone gets hurt. In such cases, the home may provide a place to retreat and find solace. The rhythm of age-old domestic activities like cooking, garden-ing, cleaning, and caring for children or pets will help renew energy and restore courage.

Unfortunately, sometimes the family is not the remedy but the cause of deep wounds and hurts. The home can be a pres-sure cooker, ready to explode with the slightest increase of heat. This is the case when there is alienation, misunderstanding, sus-picion, disloyalty, unforgiveness, untruthfulness among family members. The passage of time does not necessarily heal such hurts, but only etches them deeper into the heart. Misguided efforts to cope with these pressures may lead to alcoholism or drug dependency, adding additional burdens to the misery. Prolonged and insoluble misery pushes people to the limits of human endurance in too many cases. The fog never lifts.

Another potential source of prolonged hurt lies in religious aspirations. After years of faithful religious practice I may feel I have still not gotten anywhere in the spiritual life. I do not have the moving experiences of God that I hear others speak of and that I read of in the writings of spiritual masters. My meditation periods are still a struggle against distractions and daydreaming.

It hurts my sense of self-worth to admit that the scripture verse on prayer that I identify with most is St. Paul's confession that "we do not know how to pray as we ought" [Rom. 8:26]. It is all the more painful when other people expose their own difficulties in prayer and expect to receive expert guidance from a guide who cannot himself walk the path he sees before him. How do I cope with fog that never lifts?

Transcending Limitations

What hurts me jolts me to a sudden stop. Even a mosquito bite is enough to make me stop what I am doing and swat at the offender. What brings me to a stop is a limit. Small hurts are small limits that I can transcend fairly easily. But if life deals me a heavy blow or prolongs a limiting situation, I may stop permanently and never manage to move or grow or change again. When people find their plans rudely interrupted by failure, unexpected loss, sickness, natural or political events beyond their control, rejection, they may never recover their original motivation. Momentum once lost becomes a barrier of inertia.

Some people do find ways of going beyond the limits placed in their way. A brilliant young scientist named Stephen Hawking came down with Lou Gehrig's disease, for which there is no completely effective treatment. He is confined to a wheelchair, with slowly atrophying muscles, completely dependent on others for food, bodily necessities, and communication. He is no longer at home in the social circle of his friends and their activities. Nevertheless, he has managed to transcend this breakdown of normal functioning. Stephen Hawking's intellect is running far ahead of most people in perfect health. He computes complex equations in his head and slowly dictates them to a research assistant. He is a creative theoretician in the field of nuclear physics, astronomy, and the properties of black holes. His physical handicaps do impose severe limitations on his communication abilities, but have not impaired his intellectual creativity. Hawking has joined the elite group of people whose genius in art, literature, or science could not be stifled by severe handicaps.

The majority of us do not share their degree of creativity or their degree of suffering. But we all have our hurts, our limits. And we are all called to retain our own humanity and serve the needs of the rest of humanity as best we can in spite of our personal handicaps or oppressive situations. How each one is to progress beyond his or her limitations will be a decision that can be reached through reflective self-presence, consultation with friends, prayer, trial and error.

Youth is the time for shaping ideals and dreaming dreams, but after numerous disappointments there comes a day when I admit to myself that I will never become the great movie star, explorer, lover, author, athlete, millionaire, or artist I thought I could become. Nor am I going to be the great saint I once aspired to be. That day I quietly lay my youthful dream aside, tucking it in a bottom drawer somewhere with other items I may never use again but cherish too much to throw away. It is the day of honestly facing the reality of my human limitations. I am not the kind of person who excels, as I had assumed. I have not got it in me, or if I do, there is no opportunity for it to unfold. Like Popeye in the old comic strip, I am obliged to say, "I yam what I yam and that's all that I yam." Popeye knew he would never be much different, and did not mind if all the world knew it too. All the world is made up, anyway, of limited, imperfect human beings.

Only by going through my limits can I get past them. To accept limitedness is already to begin going beyond it, because now I can see my limits for what they are. Before, I had identified with them so closely there was no getting away. Now the act of acceptance has introduced a saving distance. I can stand back and get a better perspective. Already I am being liberated from my limitations, if only in my inward spirit. I have taken a step forward into freedom. Once I begin moving again in thought and action, I improve my vision of the horizon ahead. The divine plan for my life did not have to be revised to adjust to these changing conditions. I am moving forward according to God's original plan for me, which includes all that is capable of realization in my dream-image of myself. God works for his glory within my limitations if I can accept them patiently and even lovingly. My setbacks and reversals need to be situated in the larger plan of God's unfailing love.

Mystery of Unfailing Love

The wisdom preserved in the pages of the Old and New Testaments helps place the reality of human hurts within the mystery of God's love. In the Bible we find the cries of people who stand utterly alone with their hurts. In Jesus crucified we recognize the figure of the suffering servant of the Lord, a man of sorrows "accustomed to infirmity" [Isa. 53:3]. From his cross, the psalmist's words could be heard: "My God, my God, why have you forsaken me, far from my prayer, from the words of my cry?" [Ps. 22:2; Matt. 27:46]. The scene is reminiscent of another psalm:

> Aloud to God I cry; aloud to God, to hear me;
>   on the day of my distress I seek the Lord.
> By night my hands are stretched out without flagging;
>   my soul refuses comfort.
> When I remember God, I moan;
>   when I ponder, my spirit grows faint. [Ps. 77:2–4]

It is reminiscent also of the abandonment of Job:

> My brethren have withdrawn from me, and my friends are wholly estranged. My kinsfolk and companions neglect me, and my guests have forgotten me. . . . The young children too despise me; when I appear, they speak against me. All my intimate friends hold me in horror; those whom I loved have turned against me. [Job 19:13–19]

In the Bible, the isolation of the afflicted is reflected in several Greek and Hebrew words that convey the idea of constraint, repression, confinement in a narrow space, crushing distress. Deliverance is the opposite experience, the feeling of moving out into the open, into a broad, roomy space where one can breathe freely again. The process of being saved from crushing affliction is condensed in a few verses of Psalm 107:

> He crushed their spirit with toil;
>   when they stumbled, there was no one to help them.

They cried to the Lord in their distress;
   from their straits he rescued them.
And he led them forth from darkness and gloom
   and broke their bonds asunder.
Let them give thanks to the Lord for his kindness
   and his wondrous deeds to the children of men,
Because he shattered the gates of brass
   and burst the bars of iron. [Ps. 107:12–16]

The books of the Bible are unanimous in affirming that it is
ultimately God who saves, liberates, and heals his people's
hurts, out of his unfailing love. "The Lord is close to the bro-
kenhearted; and those who are crushed in spirit he saves. Many
are the troubles of the just man but out of them all the Lord
delivers him" [Ps. 34:19–20]. It is the Lord who rescues his
people from distress, remembers and hears them like a mother
her infant, makes them rejoice again and dance to festive tam-
bourines; see these themes in the psalms [Ps. 91:15; 9:10; 34:7,
18–19] and the prophets [Isa. 49:14–15; Jer. 31:2–5].

Nevertheless, prolonged affliction challenges my strongest
convictions about God. How could a good, merciful, and all-
powerful God allow me or any of his children to go on hurting
as atrociously as they do today in various countries? Hard as I
search, there seems to be no completely satisfying explanation
for this bottomless sea of hurting humanity. One possible reaction might be to cease believing in such a God, for it seems
monstrous to worship a God who seems to delight in the inno-
cent suffering. But the response I find most viable is to go on
believing in God's unfailing love, while recognizing that I find
God's ways incomprehensible. I could grasp, I thought, a God
who saves and heals, but that God was too small. Now I stand
once more before a larger, mysterious, incomprehensible God,
the living God. And I repeat the words of the crucified Jesus:
Into your hands, O mysterious, hidden God, I commend my
spirit, my own life and pain and all the world's hurts. My
words echo in the silence of God's mystery. Affliction draws
from the heart not only a cry of anguish but also an act of
deeper, loving trust in God's unfailing, all-embracing, mysterious love. The hurt begins to be healed when I freely surrender

to divine love in the darkness. I do not love the darkness nor the hurt, but love in the darkness and the hurt. Against all hope I cling to "the God who restores the dead to life and calls into being those things which had not been" [Rom. 4:17].

Since there are different degrees of hurts, not all of them will be immediately experienced as invitations to deepen my loving surrender to God in the darkness of faith and hope. A headache does not hurt like terminal cancer, and neither hurts like a heartache. Still, the power at work in every affliction is the power of death. On the horizon of all suffering is death. The passion of Jesus Christ teaches that suffering and death are redeemable and redemptive in the plan of God's unfailing love. Our negative, hurtful experiences convey a lesson for life and for beatitude even as they carry us toward death.

My fear of hurting often prevents me from listening to it and learning from it, or from experiencing an "overflowing joy in the midst of severe trial" [2 Cor. 8:2]. I prefer to anesthetize the hurt, do away with the immediate crisis, solve the problem as soon as possible, and get back to the frenzied, driven business I call living. But no deep lessons are learned if I always run from hurts and hardships. An illness, for example, is an inconvenience from one point of view; but from another it is an opportunity for legitimate time out to reflect and reassess my life, and to touch once more the mystery of God's unfailing love.

Sowing in Tears

A child's spontaneous reaction to being hurt is to cry. As we grow up, many of us acquire social inhibitions and hold back our tears. Women in most cultures have a time-honored permission to cry, and do so to advantage. Men cry too, but perhaps less often, less copiously, and less publicly.

In the Bible, tears flow with great abundance. Jacob wept as he wrestled with the angel [Hos. 12:5]. David and his followers "wept aloud until they could weep no more" over the pillage of Ziklag [1 Sam. 30:4], the blind Tobit cried [Tob. 3:1], Job wept on the refuse heap [Job 16:20], Jeremiah cried in secret about the exile [Jer. 13:17], and the tears of the city of Jerusalem "flow like a torrent day and night" [Lam. 2:18]. The psalmist's tears became his bread and drink [Ps. 42:4; 80:6]. He cried himself to sleep: "Every night I flood my bed with weeping; I drench my couch with my tears" [Ps. 6:7]. He hoped that the Lord would not be deaf to his tears but would record them in his book and store them in a flask [Ps. 39:13; 56:9].

In fact, God does hear prayers made with tears. "Thus says the Lord: 'Cease your cries of mourning, wipe the tears from your eyes. The sorrow you have shown shall have its reward, says the Lord'" [Jer. 31:16]. God saw the tears of King Hezekiah, agreed to heal him, and added fifteen years to his life [Isa. 38:5]. In the New Testament, the tears of the sinful woman that fell upon the feet of Jesus won her his forgiveness [Luke 7:38, 48]. The tears of Peter at the sound of the second cockcrow were the sign of his repentance. St. Augustine attributed his conversion to the tears his mother offered for seventeen years.

Why is God moved to mercy by our tears? Such tears acknowledge God as the sovereign Lord of life and death; they are a proclamation of total dependence upon God. In the parable of the tax collector and the pharisee, the tax collector assumed the posture of a man weeping, separate from the crowd, head bowed, beating his breast and saying, "O God, be merciful to me, a sinner" [Luke 18:13]. He went home from the temple justified and exultant. "Blest are you who are weeping; you shall laugh," promised Jesus [Luke 6:21].

On several occasions the gospels record the tears of Jesus. He began to weep at the death of Lazarus, which caused people to remark, "See how much he loved him" [John 11:35]. Jesus wept at the thought of the consequences of his rejection by Jerusalem: "Coming within sight of the city, he wept over it" [Luke 19:41]. The evangelists do not say that Jesus wept during his night of agony in the garden of Gethsemani, although he told his three disciples: "My heart is nearly broken with sorrow" [Matt. 26:38]. The Letter to the Hebrews is explicit about the efficacy of the tears of Jesus: "In the days when he was in the flesh, he offered prayers and supplications with loud cries and tears to God, who was able to save him from death, and he was heard because of his reverence" [Heb. 5:7].

Jesus was never described as laughing, though laughter belongs to the fullness of the human condition that Jesus embraced. Even more, laughter belongs to the time of fulfillment in the kingdom that Jesus had come to inaugurate. On the eve of his departure he promised the disciples: "Your sadness will turn into joy" [John 16:20]. His promise echoes the Old Testament theme of the return of exiles: "They departed in tears, but I will console them and guide them. . . . I will turn their mourning into joy, I will console and gladden them after their sorrows" [Jer. 31:9, 13]. Monastic tradition records examples of individuals whose aching hearts overflowed with "the gift of tears," but these monks always hoped to one day reap a harvest of consolation and gladness: "Those that sow in tears shall reap rejoicing" [Ps. 126:5].

Reaping in Joy

The hope and optimism of Christians who suffer afflictions is astounding. Some of the later New Testament writings emerged from persecuted communities. The Letter of James begins: "My brothers, count it pure joy when you are involved in every sort of trial" [James 1:2]. The First Letter of Peter proclaims: "Rejoice in the measure that you share Christ's sufferings; when his glory is revealed, you will rejoice exultantly" [1 Pet. 4:13]. Looking beyond their hurts, these believers were consoled by the victory over suffering already achieved in Christ. "You will suffer in the world," predicted Christ, "But take courage! I have overcome the world" [John 16:33].

Even more astounding is the paradox that consolation and joy can be experienced in the midst of hurt, because of Christ's victory. Joy is a Christian attitude that surfaces in every situation. The letters of St. Paul were written by a man who had gone through imprisonment, stoning, shipwreck, sickness, destitution, derision, inner uncertainty. Yet Paul could write: "Despite my many afflictions my joy knows no bounds" [2 Cor. 7:4]. He described himself as sorrowful yet always rejoicing [2 Cor. 6:10]. He praised God the Father of mercies and God of all consolation for having comforted him in all his afflictions: "As we have shared much in the suffering of Christ, so through

Christ do we share abundantly in his consolation" [2 Cor. 1:5]. Paul became so confirmed in his conviction that his hurts had a redemptive value and God's love would not leave him disappointed that he dared say: "We even boast of our afflictions!" [Rom. 5:3].

St. Paul's experience of consolation in the midst of affliction is not the exception to a rule, though his expression of it is exceptionally forceful. The same paradoxical experience could be illustrated from the lives of martyrs, both ancient and contemporary, and the lives of countless ordinary people who have suffered and still preserved their humanity and their sense of humor. The paradox is illustrated even in the folk sayings that people repeat at times of great trial and hardship: "Thank God it wasn't worse," "Every cloud has a silver lining," "It's an ill wind that blows no good." Some of the senior citizens we see sitting on porches or park benches, soothing their arthritic joints in the sunshine and watching the world go by, seem to find delight in the simple, ordinary things that pass before their gaze; they have apparently discovered a wisdom that brings them a degree of peace and pleasure even as they feel the limitations of old age.

Another dimension of being consoled in the midst of hurting can be illustrated from the life of American author Margaret Prescott Montague, who died in 1955. Suffering fine tunes the sensitivity of some people to strands of beauty and goodness they would otherwise fail to appreciate. Margaret Montague's seventy-seven years of life were an almost continual sequence of suffering that led to nearly total blindness and deafness. Emotional depression joined with physical infirmities to shake her faith in God and the goodness of life, but her faith prevailed. Her writings radiate an inner joy and peace. A particularly instructive incident occurred one day in March at a hospital where Montague was recovering from surgery. The weather was windy and partly cloudy but she was permitted to sit out on the sun porch with other patients. As she absorbed the scene around her—the people, the sparrows chirping in the trees, the periodic splashes of sunlight, and the leafless trees moving with the wind—she began to realize for the first time how wildly beautiful and joyous all creation really is. To be alive and to be part of this changing, fascinating universe seemed a precious value in spite of the hurt and anxiety she was feeling. She knew these moments were a revelation of the meaningfulness of all reality. In her own words: "I have seen life as it really is— ravishingly, ecstatically, madly beautiful, and filled to over- flowing with a wild joy, and a value unspeakable."* In later years, as she went on struggling with her afflictions, Margaret Montague recalled her experience at the hospital and drew fresh strength from the goodness and validity she had discovered at the heart of reality.

Transfigured World

The world around me often reflects back my own moods. If I am happy, the world smiles even on a drab, dull day. If I am hurting, the day will probably seem unpleasant no matter how nice it is, and people will probably seem uncooperative. If others are clearly enjoying themselves when I am hurting, I spurn their frivolous merriment because I would prefer the whole world to keep me company in my misery. Life provides enough material for anguish or for celebration at any given mo- ment, depending on the view I choose to take.

Wisdom in life seems to lie in counting on a tilt towards the better that can be discerned if one takes the broadest possible view. Horrible hurting still exists in the world side by side with undeniable goodness, beauty, purpose, and meaning, but the movement is towards the positive side. The movement may seem almost imperceptible except in the broadest perspective and the longest span of time. But in that dynamism towards the higher and better there is invincible power. Tapping that source of power can be the beginning of liberation from one's individ- ual hurts. What is individual is caught up in a universal move- ment.

---

* Anne Fremantle, ed., *The Protestant Mystics* (New York: Mentor Books, 1964), p. 261. Montague published under the name of Jane Steger as well as her own name.

St. Paul's Letter to the Romans acknowledges that the present world is enslaved to corruption and subject to futility [Rom. 8:20–21]. "All creation," observed Paul, "groans and is in agony even until now" [Rom. 8:22]. But a healing, liberating transformation is in process also; the time will come when the groans will give way to a marvelous experience of fulfillment. And so Paul could say confidently: "I consider the sufferings of the present to be as nothing compared with the glory to be revealed" [Rom. 8:14].

In John's gospel, Jesus hinted at a similar transformation using the metaphor of childbirth:

> When a woman is in labor she is sad that her time has come. When she has borne her child, she no longer remembers her pain for joy that a man has been born into the world. In the same way, you are sad for a time, but I shall see you again; then your hearts will rejoice with a joy no one can take from you [John 16:21–22].

The hurts I experience in life, and those I sympathize with in the lives of others, may be seen as part of the cosmic birthpangs that convulse all creation as it gives birth to a transfigured world. The pain is paschal, issuing in new life. There is a plan at work that is larger than any individual, and that encompasses all of history, and that nothing can frustrate. All of life's hurts, and its joys as well, can be placed against the ever-present background of this plan of God's unfailing love for the world he created and is slowly transforming into a new heaven and a new earth.

Conclusion

Pain is not a good to be loved, but neither is it something to fear and to flee in every situation. This chapter has suggested alternatives for dealing with life's inevitable hurts. Such alternatives, rooted in the Judaeo-Christian tradition, will not cure a headache as an aspirin tablet will, but they offer insights into the meaning and possible use of inevitable suffering. Because of the built-in limitations of our human condition, we are subject to physical ills and injuries, the ups and downs of changing

moods, the wear and tear of interaction with others, disappointments, accidents, and the uncertainty of surviving out-
breaks of violence. Each of us has been hurt and will be hurt
again. The hurt is real, yet we may affirm that life is fundamentally and predominantly good in all its harshness.

Because of the goodness we already enjoy in the midst of
our hurts, and because of the goodness that lies before us in the
kingdom of God, the present affliction may be at least endura-
ble. St. Paul thought the odds were entirely in our favor: "The
present burden of our trial is light enough, and earns for us an
eternal weight of glory beyond all comparison" [2 Cor. 4:17].
Paul kept his eye on the mystery concealed in affliction: the
divine plan bringing a new world to birth. In that transfigured
heaven and earth, God will be his people's glory and their joy:
"He shall wipe every tear from their eyes, and there shall be no
more death or mourning, crying out or pain, for the former
world has passed away" [Rev. 21:4]. All our hurting will be
swallowed up and forgotten in the final victory of life over
death.

Epilogue

....

The situations from daily life that have been examined in this book are the normal conditions within which the Holy Spirit of God is alive, active, and working to transform us. The Spirit may work also in more spectacular and sensational ways, but our concern in this book has been to draw attention to the divine mystery present in ordinary things. Ordinary things and experiences, because they are so commonplace, can have the effect of anesthetizing us into one-dimensional living where our spirit slowly suffocates for lack of breathing space. But we can also cultivate another attitude towards these ordinary realities of everyday experience, and learn to move through them as through a doorway into the realm of mystery leading us to unexpected possibilities of transformed living. St. Teresa of Avila, writing in Book Four of her *Interior Castle* about the mysteries hidden in the smallest creatures, said: "I believe that in each little thing created by God there is more than what is understood, even if it is a little ant." It is by being gently, attentively present to the "more than" in everything we do that we cooperate with the transforming activity of the Spirit who dwells in our hearts. In what seems ordinary and everyday there is always more than at first meets the eye. The reflections in this book have given us good practice in the art of discerning the mystery of the ordinary.